Praise for
Vector Basic Training, Second Edition

"The problem with vector images today is that I hate most of them! Mainly because something dies between the drawing and the precision vector graphic version. Perhaps it's the illustration's soul lost in the transition? Most vector images today contain too many cyber-slick gradations; they are too mathematically perfect, like many of the billions of images populating millions of microstock sites that lack anything real and human. If Von's book can help improve a designer's ability to create better vector images, I'm all for it. And remember: Just because you can make everything a gradation doesn't mean you should make everything a gradation."

— **CHARLES ANDERSON**, CSA Design

"With *Vector Basic Training*, Von Glitschka shames me. And I thank him for it. He reminds me that I am walking a tightrope of forsaking my first love: drawing. Von approaches the process with an honor and reverence that emerges from a tradition rooted in art as much as design. His depth of thought, trained hand, and ability to art direct himself have produced a stunning body of work, and he brings it all home in *VBT* to share with the reader. That's the thing with Von—not only is he a powerful talent, he's gracious enough to share it all. I'll be keeping my copy of *VBT* next to my Mac and, yes, my sketchpad."

— **TERRY MARKS**, TMARKS Design

"Von's experience as an award-winning 'illustrative designer' enables him to provide a valuable methodology for creating vector artwork guaranteed to produce results for every designer."

— **EARL GEE**, Creative Director, Gee + Chung Design

"As president of the School of Advertising Art (SAA), I would like to thank Von for writing this book. Young designers need to understand the power of the drawing process, and they need to know that time spent sketching before jumping to the computer is time well spent on any project. Von clearly demonstrates this philosophy throughout the book by incorporating interesting visual examples of his work. I am excited to share *Vector Basic Training* with SAA students."

— **JESSICA GRAVES**, President, School of Advertising Art, Kettering, Ohio

VECTOR BASIC TRAINING

A SYSTEMATIC CREATIVE PROCESS FOR BUILDING PRECISION VECTOR ARTWORK

DEVELOPED & WRITTEN BY ILLUSTRATIVE DESIGNER

VON GLITSCHKA

VECTOR BASIC TRAINING, SECOND EDITION:
A Systematic Creative Process for Building Precision Vector Artwork
Von Glitschka

New Riders

Find us on the Web at www.newriders.com
New Riders is an imprint of Peachpit, a division of Pearson Education.

To report errors, please send a note to errata@peachpit.com.

Copyright © 2016 by Glitschka Studios

Project Editor: Nikki Echler McDonald
Development Editor: Margaret S. Anderson, Stellarvisions
Production Editor: Tracey Croom
Technical Editor: Monika Gause
Copy Editor: Gretchen Dykstra
Proofreader: Kim Wimpsett
Indexer: Rebecca Plunkett
Cover Illustration: Von Glitschka, Glitschka Studios
Cover Design: Von Glitschka
Composition and Interior Design: Kim Scott, Bumpy Design
Media Producer: Eric Geoffroy

ISBN 13: 978-0-134-17673-4
ISBN 10: 0-134-17673-1

9 8 7 6 5 4 3 2 1

Printed and bound in the United States of America

To my two wonderful daughters, Savannah and Alyssa. You both inspire me in such unique and funny ways at times. I love when you two make me laugh, and seeing you both exercise your creativity is a joy to my heart. I love you both so very much, and watching you grow into caring and beautiful young women proves you're the best thing I've ever been part of creating.

—Pa

Where Are the Videos and Files?

Purchasing this book gives you access to video screencasts presenting key techniques. These videos are completely new for this edition and have detailed explanations and step-by-step demonstrations.

Throughout the book you'll see a video icon if there is a related screencast.

For certain projects there are also downloadable illustration files. By examining these files, you will be able to see all the sketches, anchor points, shapes, layers, color palettes, gradients, and detailing that I've used to create the final illustrative designs.

If you see either of these file icons, there is a design file you can download that corresponds to the illustration you see printed in the book. Most will be in Adobe Illustrator (.ai) format, but a few are Adobe Photoshop (.psd) files.

Downloading the Video and Resource Files

You can download this book's companion video and resource files from Peachpit.com using the code you'll find on the coupon at the back of this book. You can download each video segment individually or download them all at one time.

You can find step-by-step download instructions on the coupon.

Acknowledgments

The first and foremost person I need to thank is my wife, Rebecca. Her understanding and support for my work over the years is a living demonstration of caring patience and wisdom. I've spent a lot of time developing and writing this book and numerous late-night creative sessions compiling its content, and she graciously supported me every step of the way. Love you, Becky!

Peachpit acquisition editor Nikki Echler McDonald is a relentless and gentle persuader, and she has encouraged and supported me in writing this book. She also listened to my concerns and provided both answers and a shared vision. I couldn't be happier with the end result. Thanks for being patient with me, Nikki.

I'm good at creating and communicating both visual and written narratives, but that said, my grammar is hardly a work of art. Rather than paying attention during Mr. Parson's high-school English class, I spent most of my time drawing. So, I'm very thankful to have an editor like Margaret Anderson performing textual plastic surgery on my lame prose and improper use of industry nomenclature. Thanks for making me read smarter than I sound in real life, Margaret.

When it comes to the technical aspects of video production, I'm about as informed as a small neck clam. The guidance and insight I received from my Lynda.com productions helped me to record the movies for this book.

Simply put, the technical editor for this book, Monika Gause, knows Illustrator better than I ever will. When I have questions, she is the one person I know will have the answer for me. And that is why I wanted her to tech edit this book. Also, she is smart and friendly and has a cool German accent.

To everyone else on the Peachpit team, including production editor Tracey Croom and designer Kim Scott: You have a well-thought-out process that made working with you not only easy but precise. My OCD tendencies thank you. Peachpit prints the vast majority of its books, including this one, here in the United States, so I can say with complete confidence that this book was MADE IN THE USA.

To my fellow design friends with whom I shared as I created this book (you know who you are): Thank you for your willing feedback and suggestions at critical times. It helped me break through mental walls and keep moving forward on this project.

To all of you who follow me and my work on Twitter, Facebook, or my website: You've read my numerous laments and rants over the years about all manner of industry-related issues. Thank you for understanding, agreeing, sharing in return, laughing with me, laughing at me, unfollowing me, RT'ing me, forwarding my links to your friends, or posting snarky retorts telling me to chill out. This book is for you. So, stop reading this stuff and dive into the content already. Sheesh.

About the Author

Von Glitschka is principal of Glitschka Studios and has worked in the communication arts industry for more than 28 years. His work reflects the symbiotic relationship between design and illustration. This duality of skills within his own creative arsenal inspired him to coin the phrase and title "illustrative designer."

Glitschka Studios is a boutique design firm located in the Pacific Northwest. Glitschka's diverse range of illustrative design has been used by some of the most respected global brands. He's creatively collaborated with ad agencies, design firms, corporate in-house art departments, and small businesses to produce compelling results.

His exuberant graphics have garnered numerous design and illustration awards and have appeared in such publications as *Communication Arts*, *Print*, *HOW*, *Society of Illustrators* annuals, *Graphis*, *American Illustration* books, and *LogoLounge*.

Glitschka has spoken nationally at HOW Design Live, Adobe MAX, The Illustration Conference (ICON), AIGA events, ADFED groups, TEDx, SXSW, design schools, in-house art departments, and marketing groups.

His mix of humor, inspiration, great design, and solid creative methodology are all part of his engaging presentations.

You can usually find him spending an unhealthy amount of time on Twitter conversing in all manner of witty banter and sarcasm. Follow him at @vonster or visit his website at www.glitschkastudios.com.

CONTENTS

Introduction

Vector Basic Training

The one question I get asked most by other creatives is, "How do you get your vector artwork to look so nice?" When people ask me this, they're not talking about any specific art project or illustration but rather how I go about building my artwork in vector format so precisely.

The truth is that many designers, whether they're students or seasoned professionals, struggle with building precise vector shapes. I've wrestled with it myself. There are times I have to access old art files from my personal archive, and when I open them, I cringe, thinking, "Why did I build it that way?" or "That could have been done a lot better."

The point is: We all have room for improvement.

Vector Basic Training exhaustively documents my own creative process and approach to building vector artwork. The methods I'll cover in this book (with the exception of the plug-ins covered in Chapter 2) are what I'd call application-agnostic. No specific software, or version, for that matter, is required because you'll be able to use these core build methods in any vector-based application, be it Adobe Illustrator, Affinity Designer, CorelDRAW, or even Inkscape.

Illustrator may be the industry-standard application for graphic design, but there are many new choices being developed that use the same universal vector technology. The process I cover in this book will help you construct vector artwork in all of them.

For the sake of demonstration, I'll be using Illustrator, which is the current vector building application of *my* choice.

This book isn't your typical software-oriented technical manual or a how-to for using the latest tools and pull-down menu effects. It assumes you already have a general understanding of vector applications and want to improve your skills so you can build more precise vector artwork.

My creative process is systematic. You may not agree with everything I have to say, but if you apply my methods to your own creative endeavors over time, you'll be pleased with the results.

Why Designers Should Draw

Yes, this is a book about vector build methods, but its creative foundation is core drawing skills—something I stress repeatedly because I feel so strongly about their importance to the creative process.

We all drew pictures freely and joyfully when we were children, with arms and legs protruding madly from the heads of our very first crudely rendered self-portraits. Many of you continued to draw as you grew older, and that creative passion is probably one of the main reasons you're involved in graphic arts today.

Some of you, however, didn't stick with drawing and have evolved into a designer who can't, or simply doesn't, draw. This is unacceptable.

If you drew every day, in five years you certainly would not say to yourself, "I wish I never would have started drawing again. I am a worse designer now." Your creative skills will only improve by integrating drawing into your creative process. The practical benefits of drawing will be self-evident and a lot of fun.

I should point out that when I say "drawing," I don't mean that everyone needs to become a full-fledged illustrator. Being able to draw allows you to take the ethereal concept in your mind and formulate it visually. The more you draw, the better you're able to capture and leverage ideas and expand your creative potential. Combine improved drawing skills with the vector build methods in this book, and you will definitely execute better artwork with more precision.

Our industry, more than most, is in constant flux because of the ever-changing technologies we work with. At times, keeping up to speed with everything can be overwhelming, but doing so is essential to staying creatively relevant with the larger design community.

A creative process should be flexible enough to accommodate new technology, methods, and tools that will improve its efficiency without compromising its effectiveness.

A good example of this is drawing on an iPad or a tablet instead of using paper and a pencil or pen. It exercises the same creative muscles, and you have the flexibility of digital as well.

This book won't cover every possible tool for building vector art in Illustrator, but it will introduce you to an easy-to-understand creative process that you can use to create high-quality design work, regardless of which vector program you use.

Along the way, I'll touch on additional tools and techniques that make certain vector builds easier to accomplish. My methodology may stretch your creative comfort zone, but unless you adapt to new methods and constantly strive to improve your design skills, you risk becoming a dreaded *design-o-saur*, and your once forward-looking design work will start to resemble a thing of the past.

So don't fossilize your creative potential. Take time to read through this book and you'll discover a creative workflow that will greatly enhance your vector creations.

FIELD NOTES

A Systematic Creative Process

Having a plan of creative attack as you approach any given design project is essential in order to produce work that is both appropriate and effective for your clients. Here's how my creative process breaks down into specific stages:

1. Do research.

2. Select a style.

3. Create thumbnail sketches.

4. Refine the sketches.

5. Build the artwork.

6. Finalize the artwork.

Vector Basic Training will serve as your field guide to creative excellence, covering all these topics and more, so you'll be better equipped to approach your own work and grow your skills moving forward.

CHAPTER 1

Bézier Curves: A Brief History

My first year at Lydia Hawk Elementary School was the last year first-grade teacher Mrs. Jerkins would teach before retiring. In hindsight, I can see she was a mean-spirited grouch who was way past due for retirement. She also bore a striking resemblance to "The Church Lady" from the famous *Saturday Night Live* skit. At the time, of course, I didn't think that. I just thought this was what school was all about because I had nothing else to compare it to.

Fear of Math

I remember the day like it was yesterday. Mrs. Jerkins called me up to the chalkboard to solve a math problem. As was her practice, she stood scowling off to the side of the chalkboard as I approached. In one hand, she held a rubber-tipped wooden dowel, and in the other, she gripped a chain that hung from an intercom speaker with which she could call the office in one quick, furious pull.

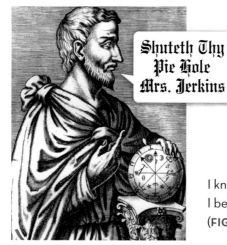

For what seemed like an eternity, I stood with my face a few inches from the chalkboard, staring at the math problem with no clue of how to solve it. Nervously, I turned to Mrs. Jerkins and asked, "How do I do it?"

She furrowed her brow and angrily slapped the wooden dowel against the chalkboard, shouting, "Solve the problem or I call the office!"

I knew I couldn't give her the correct answer. Frustrated, I began to cry. From that point forward, I loathed math (**FIGURE 1.1**). It scared me.

FIGURE 1.1 I suppose Pythagoras might have taken issue with Mrs. Jerkins for giving math such a bum rap in my mind.

Math Is Cool

Throughout the remainder of my school years, I both feared and loathed math. When I started thinking about college, I chose art school because I loved art and was excited by the possibility of drawing and creating art for a living. But, to be honest, I also thought to myself, "Art school won't have any math classes!"

But, as some kids learn to like Brussels sprouts, sushi, and a well-aged cheese plate as they grow older, I've learned to appreciate math. In fact, I think it's pretty cool. Over the years, I've come to realize just how much math is a part of everything we experience in life. And, the more I've learned about building vector shapes with Bézier curves, the more I've come to appreciate the geometric equations that underlie all digital art.

Even though I'm not that great at math myself—my daughter's fourth-grade homework has been known to stump me—math no longer scares the bejeezus out of me. In fact, I think it's pretty cool. And whether or not you or I fully comprehend the mechanics of math, I can fully appreciate knowing we should understand that it's behind all of the digital art we create.

Who Created Bézier Curves?

I won't pretend to be an expert in math history, but I've done enough sleuthing to trace the family history of the modern Bézier curve, which forms the basis of every vector drawing program in use today. Understanding this history won't improve your drawing- or vector-building skills, but it will give you a better appreciation of the digital tools we take for granted.

The Vector Family Tree

Mathematics is an ever-expanding knowledge base driven by fertile minds. One person's work in the field has historically enabled the next generation to advance. The vector family tree that fruited the Bézier curve sprouted from this same form of progressive development, by way of four key individuals:

- **Karl Weierstrass** (1815–1897): This German mathematician created the Weierstrass theorem, which stated (in very basic terms) that any function or set of data points can be modeled with a polynomial. A polynomial is an algebraic equation that sounds scary but is actually the vector artist's best buddy. Suffice it to say that simple polynomials are easy to graph, as they produce smooth and continuous curves or lines. Sound familiar?

- **Sergei Natanovich Bernstein** (1880–1968): This Jewish Soviet mathematician proved the Weierstrass theorem through his own namesake, Bernstein polynomials.

- **Paul de Casteljau** (1930–1999): A French physicist and mathematician who worked for the carmaker Citroën. De Casteljau used Bernstein's polynomials to develop the de Casteljau algorithm (a step-by-step solution to figure out a problem) for computing Bézier curves, which enabled Citroën to accurately create more beautiful curves in its vehicles (**FIGURE 1.2**).

- **Pierre Bézier** (1910–1999): A French contemporary of Paul de Casteljau, Bézier was an engineer who worked for the car manufacturer Renault. He is directly responsible for patenting and popularizing Bézier curves within a digital context through the development of CAD/CAM software, and because of that, Bézier curves bear his name (**FIGURE 1.3**).

Before the development of Bézier curves, it was impossible to create smooth curves on early CAD/CAM systems. As the technology improved in the 1970s and 1980s, it appeared in Illustrator and then in FreeHand.

Personally, I think de Casteljau got shafted on the legacy end of things. After all, he was the rightful inventor. But, then again, "de Casteljau curve" just doesn't roll off the tongue as easy as "Bézier curve."

Bézier curves might be math-driven, but it was the design thinkers who breathed life into those equations and used them to form something beautiful.

FIGURE 1.2 Paul de Casteljau used Bézier curves to create well-rounded car designs for Citroën.

FIGURE 1.3 My illustration of Pierre Bézier, a.k.a. "The French Curve."

As much as I think analog methods, such as drawing, are vital to the creative process, I can't imagine doing my job without my digital tools. I'm a geek: I love my Mac and the way it supports my creative workflow.

We can all thank Pierre Bézier for taking Bézier curves from analog to digital, making Bézier curves as ubiquitous in the design industry as black clothes and designer frames.

What Is a Bézier Curve?

So what does the mathematical equation of a Bézier curve look like? I asked Bill Casselman, professor of mathematics at the University of British Columbia, to give us a peek at a basic Bézier curve and the math behind it (**FIGURE 1.4**).

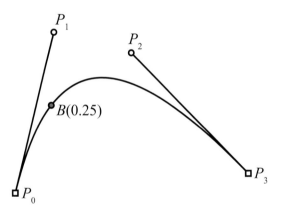

FIGURE 1.4 A basic Bézier curve and its mathematical equation, created by Dr. Bill Casselman.

$$B(t) = (1 - t)^3 P_0 + 3(1 - t)^2 t P_1 + 3(1 - t)t^2 P_2 + t^3 P_3$$

You'd probably have an easier time learning to speak Klingon than trying to wrap your brain around the math required to create a Bézier curve. Thanks to Pierre Bézier, you'll never have to. All you really need to know is that vector art is made up of anchor points and paths and that a Bézier curve is any segment of that path between two anchor points that requires a curved shape. One piece of art can have thousands of Bézier curves in it, as shown in **FIGURE 1.5**.

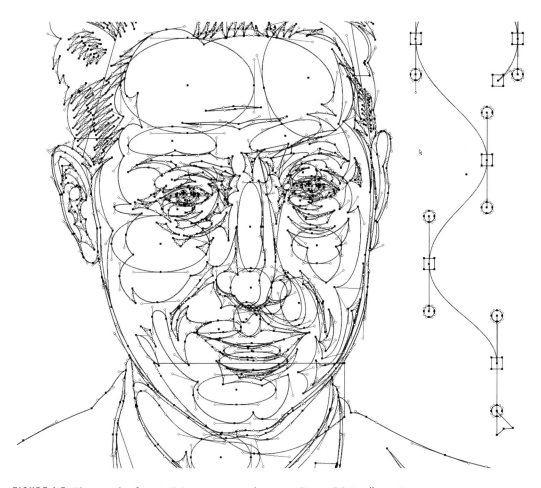

FIGURE 1.5 Thousands of ironic Bézier curves make up my Pierre Bézier illustration.

Put even more simply, a Bézier curve is a path that you can bend from one end or the other using the handlebars extended from the anchor points at each end of the path.

When to Use a Bézier Curve

Odds are good that if your vector design has curves in it, you'll be using Bézier curves to build it. A Bézier curve has handlebars that protrude out of its various anchor points. You use these to control and manipulate the curves to create the exact shapes you need. The more organic and free-form your design is, the more likely you'll need to manipulate Bézier curves to build the vector shapes. It's impossible to create graceful forms without them (**FIGURE 1.6**).

That said, you won't need to use Bézier curves for every project. For example, if you're creating an image that's chunky and graphic—without smooth curves—you can use just anchor points and paths. I didn't need to grab the handlebars at all when creating **FIGURE 1.7** (that said, see the Field Notes on the next page).

Knowing when to use a Bézier curve—and when not to—has a lot to do with what you're creating. Chapter 6, "Vector Build Methods," goes into more detail about vector build methods and how they can help *or* hinder your art.

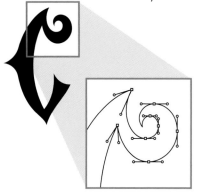

FIGURE 1.6 This funky C uses nothing but Bézier curves and handles.

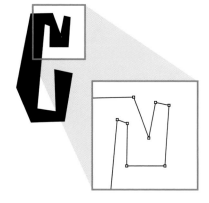

FIGURE 1.7 This chunky, graphic C uses no Bézier curves, so no handlebars were needed.

A Beautiful Irony

The use of Bézier curves in vector-based graphic programs has transformed the digital industry. You can now take your pen-and-paper ideas and build them precisely using digital tools. And because vector art is resolution independent, you can scale your work to any size without degrading its quality—that makes repurposing your work easier than ever before.

It was math that revealed the Bézier curve, but it was artists (many of whom were likely math-phobic) who took those curves and who can now use them to tell fantastic visual stories.

It's a beautiful irony, and for that I say, "Vive Bézier!"

FIELD NOTES

Vector Detailing Trick

When you create artwork that's chunky, like the C in Figure 1.7, you *can* build it without the use of Bézier curves, but even on art like this I'd recommend building it with subtle ones. Add a shallow curve between the anchor points so that the line isn't absolutely straight.

This is a method I use to improve the visual aesthetics of my design work. Simply using a computer to create art runs the risk of creating work that's too perfect, too straight, too sterile.

Infusing my design with these delicate Bézier curves makes the final form appear more natural and less computerized— more authentic, if you will.

DESIGN DRILLS:
Behind the Vector Curtain

When you're working in Adobe Illustrator, you can toggle between Preview and Outline modes (Command-Y or Control-Y) to see the raw vector work behind your design. Flipping to Outline mode is a fast and easy way to see how Bézier curves make vector art possible.

In fact, the earliest version of Illustrator forced you to build all of your art in Outline mode. You could only take sneak peeks using Preview to visually gauge your progress. But then you'd have to revert to Outline mode to continue building or editing your vectors.

When you're in Outline mode, none of the artwork is anti-aliased. It's simply a black-and-white bitmapped preview of the paths. So if you zoom in on a path, you'll see the individual stair steps or pixels that form the curvature of that path displayed on your monitor.

This all changed when another vector program, Aldus FreeHand, was released. It allowed you to build in Preview mode, which made the whole process far easier and more intuitive. Eventually, Illustrator adopted the same modus operandi.

Let's take a peek behind the vector curtain and view the Bézier curves of two designs from my project archives (**FIGURE 1.8** through **FIGURE 1.11**). I've selected these because they represent two distinctly different styles and project types. Styles and project types vary, but the fundamental Bézier curve structure behind them all works the same. The project shown in **FIGURE 1.9** takes far more Bézier curves to pull off than a simple style like the one in **FIGURE 1.11**. The more shapes within a design, the more Bézier curves your art will have.

FIGURE 1.8 The raw Bézier curves for an illustration titled "Body & Soul." A complex illustration like this one contains numerous vector shapes and can look pretty chaotic when viewed in its raw Bézier curve glory. But in reality, each anchor point and path is in its proper location.

FIGURE 1.9 The final "Body & Soul" illustration, created in the segmented style, accompanied a feature article in a women's health magazine.

FIGURE 1.10 What's missing in this design? Answer: straight lines. All of the raw vector paths within this tribal-styled design depend solely on Bézier curves to form the elegant shapes that make up the balanced design.

FIGURE 1.11 This design, created in the tribal style, was used as an art print and on products such as the pillow shown here.

CHAPTER 2

Your Creative Armament

I've been creating vector artwork and wrangling with Bézier curves for well over two decades now. For fourteen of those years, I was a die-hard Macromedia FreeHand user. Along the way, I'd use Adobe Illustrator from time to time—you know, if I *had* to. But when Adobe bought FreeHand, I saw the writing on the wall and committed myself to an exclusive relationship with Illustrator. We haven't always gotten along, Illustrator and I, but our creative relationship deepens and improves with each passing software release.

A Love-Hate Relationship

It's hard to use something day in and day out—especially something so closely tied to my personal passion for creativity—without becoming somewhat fanatical about it. Let me start by saying that I *love* how Adobe Illustrator makes it so easy for me to turn my designs into precise, well-built vector illustrations.

However, as much as I appreciate Illustrator's many fine qualities, there are times when it drives me absolutely nuts. (Some of you may be nodding your heads in agreement.) Years ago, I wrote a blog post about my "switcher" frustrations and in the process coined the phrase "Adobe Frustrator." Adobe's lead marketing director for Illustrator at that time saw my post, agreed with many of my criticisms, and invited me to be on the Illustrator beta team. I've been part of that team since the release of Illustrator CS3 and have directly consulted on a handful of new tools and features over the years since. So, as you can see, I've been involved in the software's development for a long time.

After several years of working with Illustrator and contributing to its development as a beta tester, I still have some big gripes about its functionality, and I'll touch on these throughout this chapter. That said, the program has much improved since I first started using it, and it still is the industry standard for vector design and illustration.

Whether you use Illustrator, Affinity Designer, CorelDraw, Impulse, Inkscape—or any other app from an ever-growing list of open source vector programs—before you can control Bézier curves and build vector art successfully, you must become familiar with your core building tools. All of these programs use Bézier curves for vector building. Illustrator and other apps are often called vector-drawing programs, but it would be more accurate to call them vector-building programs, because they let you build shapes via anchor points and paths. The difference among programs lies in the additional proprietary tools provided to manipulate points and paths.

For ease of communication, this book uses Adobe Illustrator to show-case the creative process. In this chapter, I'll tell you about the twelve core Illustrator tools I use to build precise vector graphics. If you don't have Illustrator, eleven of these tools will have equivalents in the other vector programs. The one exception is the VectorScribe plug-in from Astute Graphics. This exists only for Illustrator. This plug-in isn't manda-tory; it just makes the process faster. I'll show you how to create with and without this plug-in.

Vector building can be accomplished in any vector-based program. The tools may have different names and might not work exactly the same way, but they should all enable you to arrive at the same precise solution. The key to success as an illustrative designer is to get back to basics. A sound and systematic creative process that includes analog drawing at its core will improve your ability to execute digital art at a higher level.

Core Tools for Vector Building

Illustrator is replete with an array of tools that grows with each new soft-ware release. Whole books are dedicated to documenting these new tools and how to use them. This book, however, is dedicated to basic training, so I'll simplify the process by focusing on only the tools you need to create precise vector shapes within any given drawing program.

The Twelve Disciples of Design

Each of the twelve tools listed here serves a specific function in the build process. Keep in mind that some of these tools lend themselves to specific build methods, which are covered in more detail in Chapter 6, "Vector Build Methods."

The following are the twelve core tools you'll use to create precise vector shapes:

1. **Pen tool** (P): Precise vector building wouldn't be possible without the Pen tool. You'll use it to lay down all of your anchor points, one by one, forming a path that makes the vector shape you need (**FIGURE 2.1**).

2. **Add Anchor Point tool** (+): This tool lets you add an additional anchor point to any path you've created (**FIGURE 2.2**).

3. **Delete Anchor Point tool** (–): This tool removes any anchor point from any path without breaking the path (**FIGURE 2.3**). But this tool is really useful only on straight paths; if you remove a point on a curved path, it ruins the path's shape. I'll explain this in more detail in Chapter 6.

FIGURE 2.1 Pen tool.

FIGURE 2.2 Add Anchor Point tool.

You can also select one or more anchor points and click "Remove selected anchor points" from the Control panel menu at the top of the screen. The results are exactly the same either way.

4. **Convert Anchor Point tool** (Shift-C): This tool converts smooth points to corner points. It can also reveal, isolate, manipulate, and/or retract handlebars independently to adjust a Bézier curve (**FIGURE 2.4**). You can also use this tool to reshape the segment of a path (**FIGURE 2.5**). This feature is in Creative Cloud 2014 and above only.

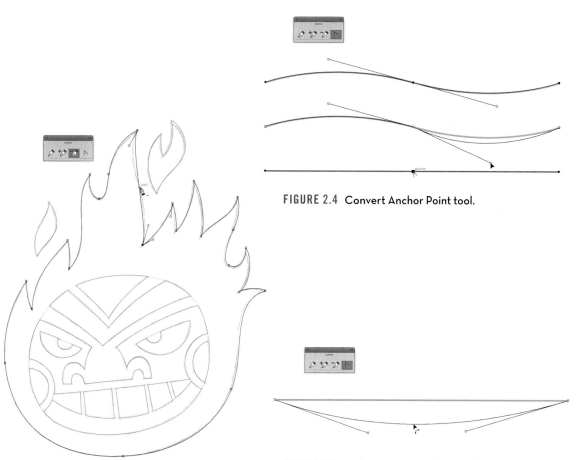

FIGURE 2.4 Convert Anchor Point tool.

FIGURE 2.3 Delete Anchor Point tool.

FIGURE 2.5 Path Segment Reshape with the Convert Anchor Point.

5. **Selection tool** (V): This tool scales objects larger or smaller when bounding box is visible. It also lets you click or drag to select shapes as individual objects and manipulate handlebars to adjust a Bézier curve (**FIGURE 2.6**).

6. **Direct Selection tool** (A): This tool lets you directly click or drag to select a specific segment of a path or individual anchor points. It can also reveal, isolate, and manipulate handlebars to adjust a Bézier curve (**FIGURE 2.7**).

7. **Rectangle tool** (M): This tool creates complete shapes with 90-degree angles (**FIGURE 2.8**). For more information, see "Shape-Building Method" in Chapter 6.

8. **Ellipse tool** (L): This tool creates complete circular or elliptical shapes (**FIGURE 2.9**). For more information, see "Shape-Building Method" in Chapter 6.

9. **Pathfinder tool** (Shift-Command-F9 or Shift-Control-F9): This tool lets you build shapes (think cookie cutters) using its Unite, Minus Front, Intersect, and Exclude modes (**FIGURES 2.10–2.13**). There are other functions within the tool, but I'll focus on these four.

FIGURE 2.6 Selection tool.

FIGURE 2.7 Direct Selection tool.

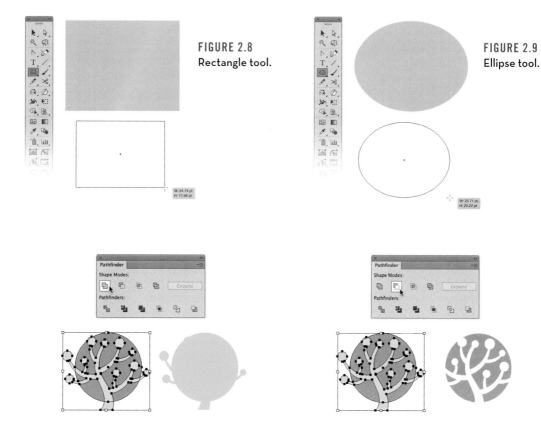

FIGURE 2.8
Rectangle tool.

FIGURE 2.9
Ellipse tool.

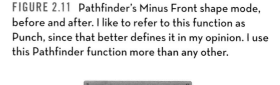

FIGURE 2.10 Pathfinder's Unite shape mode, before and after. I use this feature a lot when shape building my artwork.

FIGURE 2.11 Pathfinder's Minus Front shape mode, before and after. I like to refer to this function as Punch, since that better defines it in my opinion. I use this Pathfinder function more than any other.

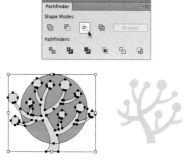

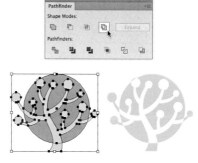

FIGURE 2.12 Pathfinder's Intersect shape mode, before and after.

FIGURE 2.13 Pathfinder's Exclude shape mode, before and after. Personally, I never use this function.

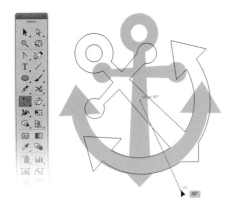

FIGURE 2.14 Rotate tool.

10. **Rotate tool** (R): This tool lets you define the rotating axis of any selected object and rotate it on the fly or via a specific numerical amount (**FIGURE 2.14**).

11. **Reflect tool** (O): This tool lets you flip a selected object horizontally or vertically. You'll use it mainly for creating symmetrical designs (**FIGURE 2.15**). For more information, see "Symmetry Is Your Friend" in Chapter 6.

12. **VectorScribe plug-in** (Astute Graphics): This plug-in makes editing and forming your final vector shapes far easier and more precise than Illustrator's own tools (Convert Anchor Point tool, Shift-C). The plug-in includes six tools (**FIGURE 2.16**), but I'll focus on two: PathScribe and Dynamic Corners. It also includes a function called Smart Remove Point.

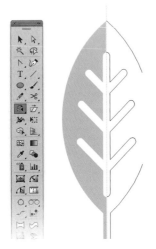

FIGURE 2.15 Reflect tool. Click the central anchor point on your shape and reflect it to form the whole piece of artwork. I'll cover this type of symmetry in Chapter 6.

FIGURE 2.16 The VectorScribe plug-in includes the Dynamic Shapes tool, Dynamic Corners tool, PathScribe tool, Dynamic Measure tool, Extend Path tool, Smart Remove Brush tool, and Smart Remove Point function.

VectorScribe Plug-in

When I first discovered the VectorScribe plug-in, I knew I'd found the Holy Grail of vector building. Simply put, it has fundamentally transformed how I approach my vector artwork because of its extremely intuitive and customizable tools.

I used to love FreeHand because it made building and editing anchor points and paths quicker and easier than Illustrator did, with fewer tools and less hassle. When I switched to Adobe Illustrator, my build time slowed down.

The whole reason I use the VectorScribe plug-in is because it lets me build faster and with greater ease than I could using Illustrator's own tools and functions. In fact, VectorScribe works so well that I can build even faster and with more precision than I did when I used FreeHand.

That said, the methodology I cover in this book doesn't require a plug-in to use it. You could choose not to use the plug-ins and still manage to create your vector artwork using only the tools available in Illustrator. It'll just take you a lot longer, and you won't be able to customize your workflow to the degree the plug-ins allow.

Since I'm covering only two of the six tools included in the VectorScribe plug-in, I encourage you to experiment with the others on your own. Astute Graphics has developed other helpful plug-ins for Illustrator that I use in my own daily workflow that I haven't covered in this book, so make sure to check them all out at www.astutegraphics.com.

My Three Amigos

VectorScribe's PathScribe and Dynamic Corners tools and its Smart Remove Point function—which I fondly refer to as my three amigos—are essential to precise building:

1. **PathScribe tool**: This tool lets you grab a vector path anywhere (between two anchor points) and bend it into any free-form shape (**FIGURE 2.17**).

2. **Dynamic Corners tool**: With this tool you can select any corner anchor point and round it off. Because it's dynamic, you can go back at any time to adjust or remove the rounding (**FIGURE 2.18**).

3. **Smart Remove Point**: This feature allows you to select an anchor point and delete it without destroying the original shape of your vector path (**FIGURE 2.19**). I'll cover this function and another called Remove Redundant Point in more depth in Chapter 6.

  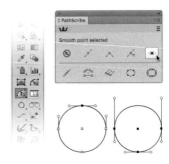

FIGURE 2.17 With the PathScribe tool you simply grab a vector path anywhere between two anchor points and bend the Bézier curve into the specific shape needed to match your drawing. Simply push and pull your paths to form them into your final art (like vector clay, if you will). The functionality is simple, is intuitive, and, most importantly, leads to precise vector building.

FIGURE 2.18 The Dynamic Corners tool lets you round off any type of path. You can even go back later to adjust it or remove it. It's jaw-droppingly easy to use and superior to Illustrator's corner widget feature.

FIGURE 2.19 The Smart Remove Point function lives up to its name. It can smartly remove an anchor point from a path without destroying the path's overall shape. I cover all of the plugin features in more depth in the video included with this book.

Customize Your Environment

Every vector-drawing program comes with default settings. In general, the defaults are OK, but customizing your preferences will make creating your vector graphics a lot easier. The following customizations are geared for Illustrator. Look for equivalent controls and features in the drawing application of your choice.

My Preference for Preferences

You'll want to customize these three areas:

- **Preferences/General**: The settings shown in **FIGURE 2.20** will help you make adjustments to your art as you work and scale properly when resizing.

- **Preferences/Selection & Anchor Display**: The settings shown in **FIGURE 2.21** make it easier to notice and isolate problem areas in your vector shapes. They also help you build precise Bézier curves by editing and adjusting the anchor points and the handles that control the paths.

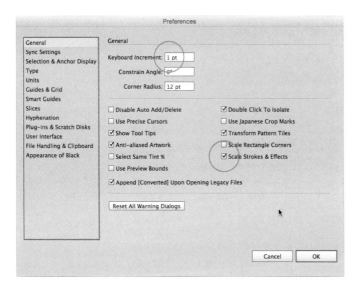

FIGURE 2.20 Preferences > General: Keep Keyboard Increment set at 1 point or lower. Make sure you have Scale Strokes & Effects checked.

- **Preferences/Smart Guides**: The settings shown in **FIGURE 2.22** will let you use Smart Guides to assist you as you build. This will help you know when you're hovering over an anchor point in a path that isn't selected, for example. It will also deactivate some features that can get in the way while you build.

FIGURE 2.21 Preferences > Selection & Anchor Display: Select the largest display for your Anchors and Handles (the ones featuring the handles with hollow ends). Check "Show handles when multiple anchors are selected." Check "Enable Rubber Band for Pen and Curvature Tool" as well—this will help you as you build using the pen tool. If you're using the VectorScribe Plug-in, then make sure to input 3° in the "Hide Corner Widget for angles greater than" box. This will prevent them from displaying. You can also toggle this on and off by going to View > Hide Corner Widget.

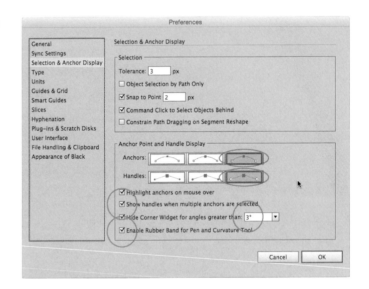

FIGURE 2.22 Preferences > Smart Guides: Make sure you uncheck Alignment Guides. And set Snapping Tolerance to 3 pt. or lower. I uncheck Alignment Guides because the program tries to associate everything you build with other elements in your file whether you want it to or not, and this can become highly annoying as you build vector shapes. I turn off Construction Guides for the same reason.

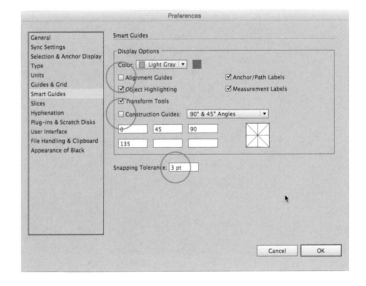

Keyboard Shortcuts and Actions

Illustrator's customizable keyboard commands and actions are, in my opinion, two of the app's most underrated features. Most people never even tap into them.

Keyboard shortcuts are just what they sound like: the ability to use a key command instead of hunting down the command in a drop-down menu. They help make your workflow more efficient.

Not all functions in Illustrator let you add a shortcut command, though. In those cases, actions are your best bet. Actions allow you to record multiple keyboard commands, dialog box entries, or menu choices. You can even choose a specific keyboard shortcut to trigger your action. The end result lets you push one button to run a series of commands instantly, which obviously saves time. The best way to determine how you can best use actions is to simply experiment. Anything you do routinely is a good candidate for an action.

For example, I have an action that converts all text to paths and then saves my artwork as a PDF onto my desktop so I can email a design to a client. It's all about streamlining mundane tasks.

To create your own keyboard shortcuts, go to Edit > Keyboard Shortcuts > Select and pick either the Tools or Menu command from the drop-down menu in the pop-up window. Select a specific tool or menu command and then enter the key you want the task to be assigned to. Illustrator will tell you if the key is already assigned, and you can decide to ignore or override it. Click Save, and your keyboard shortcut is ready to use. It's that simple.

To create an action, go to Window > Actions. On the Actions panel, click the fly-out menu in the top-right corner. Then click New Action. In the pop-up window that opens, name your action, assign it to an action set (mine is GS Actions), bind your action to an F key, and click Record > Proceed to compile the series of commands you want to record (**FIGURE 2.23**). (Remember that not all functions in Illustrator are recordable.) Once done, click Stop in the Actions palette. You now have a customized action at the ready.

FIGURE 2.23 To create the Clone shortcut, from the Actions menu, choose New Action. Next, record yourself copying a shape (Command-C or Control-C) and then pasting it in front (Command-F or Control-F). Stop recording. You have now assigned a Clone keyboard shortcut to the F3 key.

Make sure to save your action set by going to the fly-out menu in the top-right corner of the Actions panel and clicking Save Actions. I also recommend saving a copy of your actions to another location outside of the application folder because if you ever have to re-install illustrator, you'll lose them.

How you ultimately use these features will depend greatly on what type of work you'll be creating, but when it comes to building vector graphics, I have customized a handful of commands to make routine tasks easier. Here are twelve shortcuts and two actions I've assigned to function keys in order to simplify my workflow and save time:

- **F1** is Make Clipping Mask (Command-7 or Control-7).

- **F2** is Release Clipping Mask (Option-Command-7 or Alt-Control-7).

- **F3** is Clone. Illustrator has no clone command. To clone an object, you must copy a shape (Command-C or Control-C) and then paste it in front (Command-F or Control-F). That's two commands and four keys to hit. Keyboard shortcuts don't allow multiple commands, so you'll need to record an action and bind it to a function key (Figure 2.23).

- **F4** is Send to Back (Shift-Command-[or Shift-Control={).

- **F5** is Bring to Front Again (Shift-Command-] or Shift-Control-]).

- **F6** is Ungroup (Shift-Command-G or Shift-Control-G).

- **F7** is Unite. This lets me unite two individual shapes into one without moving my cursor to the Pathfinder panel. Since the Pathfinder panel functions don't have keyboard commands, I created an action for this function and assigned it to the F7 key.

- **F8** is Deselect All (Shift-Command-A or Shift-Control-A). Sometimes when you're zoomed into your design, you can't click the artboard to deselect an object. Assigning the Deselect shortcut to the F8 key is like killing three keys with one click.

- **F9** is Punch (Minus Front). Using this I can select two shapes, one on top of the other, and, like a cookie cutter, punch out the top shape from the bottom shape with one button push. Since the Pathfinder panel functions don't have keyboard commands, I created an action for this function and assigned it to the F9 key.

- **F10** is Place Image. Since Illustrator's place command requires three keys (Shift-Command-P), I've utilized the F10 key to streamline this function. Almost everything I create in Illustrator is based on a drawing, so this is how I get my refined sketches into the vector-building environment with one key press instead of three.

- **Option-F1** is Select Same Fill Color. I use this to quickly select vector elements with the same fill attributes.

- **Option-F2** is Select Same Stroke Color. I use this to quickly select vector elements with the same stroke attributes.

Stop Re-creating the Wheel

When you begin a new project, you should be able to start building immediately. You shouldn't have to waste time setting preferences, importing graphic styles and color swatch libraries, creating new layer structures, and so on, at the start of each and every project. I save myself a ton of time by creating a new document profile in Illustrator that makes my favorite settings the default for each new document I create.

In this section, I'll show you how to set the foundation for a creative process that lets you spend less time fussing with your computer and more time producing great designs.

Create a New Document Profile

Creating a new document profile in Illustrator is a simple three-step process:

1. **Create a new document** (Command-N or Control-N). In the New Document dialog, select the general properties you want, name the file, and click OK (**FIGURE 2.24**).

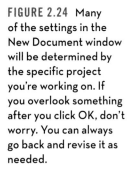

FIGURE 2.24 Many of the settings in the New Document window will be determined by the specific project you're working on. If you overlook something after you click OK, don't worry. You can always go back and revise it as needed.

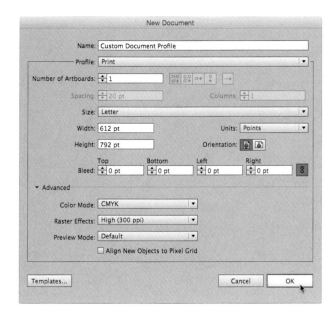

2. **Customize your properties.** In your new document, set up properties in the way you like to work. Maybe you prefer rules to always be visible, specific colors to be loaded in your swatches panel, and so on. It's up to you. All of the resource files provided with this book reflect my preferred document profile. (We'll go over three essential properties that you should include in your new document profile in "Set Graphic Styles for Building" later in this chapter.)

3. **Save your startup profile** (Command-S or Control-S). Once you have your file set up with all the properties you want, it's time to save it. On a Mac, go to File > Save (Command-S) and save your startup profile in this location: User/Library/Application Support/Adobe/ Adobe Illustrator Version/Language/New Document Profiles.

   On a PC, go to File > Save (Control-S) and save your startup profile in this location: User > AppData > Roaming > Adobe > Adobe Illustrator Version Settings > Language > x64 > New Document Profiles.

From this point forward, your new profile will appear in the New Document dialog (**FIGURE 2.25**). You can simply select it and get straight to work.

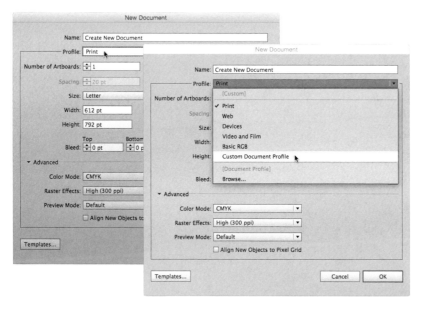

FIGURE 2.25 This is how your startup profile is listed in the New Document pull-down menu when you're creating a new document.

When you begin a new project using your customized new document profile, you can focus on the creative work rather than the tools needed to pull it off. Saving specific profiles for specific types of work you do on a regular basis will help you be more efficient and allow you to spend more time on actual creative work and less on file management.

Read on to learn about ways to speed up your vector build times.

Set Graphic Styles for Building

Two primary tasks define the creative process described in this book: drawing and building. You'll draw out your art, scan it in, and then build it within Illustrator or whatever application you prefer. Drawing is the creative foundation on which you build.

Prior to starting the building process, you'll want to create two simple graphic styles and save them in your new document profile. These determine your working line weight and color during the build process. To create a graphic style, just create any shape with any fill or stroke color and width you want and drag it into the Graphic Styles palette. Done.

When I scan in a drawing that will form the basis of a digital illustration, the scan shows up in black and white, and then I reduce its opacity so it becomes my guide for building. By setting my default line styles to magenta, the colored lines pop off the background, and I can clearly see what I'm creating. Use whatever color you want as long as it's not black, which would be too hard to see (**FIGURE 2.26**).

FIGURE 2.26 My default graphic style is a .5 pt. magenta-colored stroke. I also have a secondary graphic style that is a .25 pt. magenta-colored stroke. These help me easily see what I'm creating.

As you build your vector art, you'll zoom in and out so you can see certain portions better. When I'm zoomed out, I use the .5 pt. stroke graphic style, and when I'm zoomed in I use the .25 pt. stroke graphic style. Using a .5 pt. stroke when zoomed in produces a line that's too fat, which makes it hard to analyze contoured shapes as you build. Using a .25 pt. stroke when zoomed out does the opposite: the line is too thin and hard to see.

Of course, depending on your monitor's resolution, you might prefer to use a different weight for your graphic styles. Experiment and figure out what works best for you.

Enable Smart Guides for Building

I highly recommend that you enable Smart Guides (Command-U or Control-U) as you build your artwork. Smart Guides make snapping to points and paths more obvious. Without them, it's easy to think something is snapped into the correct location only to find out later that it's slightly off.

Smart Guides also help you select items with more precision and provide live pop-up information when you rotate items or hover over content in your document (**FIGURE 2.27**).

Using Smart Guides is a balancing act, however. I find myself toggling them on and off throughout the creative process because they can sometimes get in the way or force a snap when you don't want it.

If you're not used to working with these guides turned on, I suggest you get used to it. The benefits outweigh the annoying UI behavior.

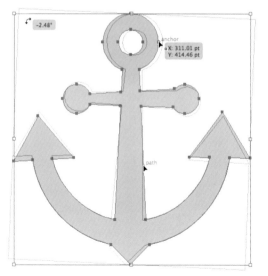 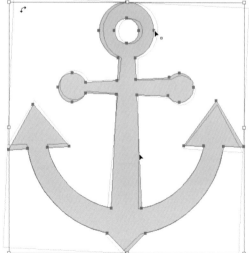

FIGURE 2.27 Left: With Smart Guides enabled, you can select a point or path or rotate a selected object. Smart Guides also give you dynamic information that changes based on which tool you're using and which shape you mouse over. Right: With Smart Guides turned off, a selected point, path, or rotated object displays no information.

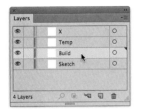

FIGURE 2.28 I begin every project with four layers: storage (which I name X), temp, build, and sketch.

Establish a Layer Structure for Building

For whatever reason, Adobe has decided that layer information isn't worthy of being one of the properties you can add to a new document profile. This is highly annoying and should be added to a future version of the software, in my humble opinion.

For now, you have to establish layers manually. Whether I'm working on a logo design, character illustration, or pattern design, I follow the same hierarchy when it comes to layering (**FIGURE 2.28**). I start with four layers: storage (which I name X), temp, build, and sketch.

From the top down, my layers are as follows:

1. **Storage (which I name X)**: As I build artwork, I tend to experiment. So I make copies of elements and move them to my X layer, which is not visible. I also make a copy of all of my paths before I start coloring and put those in the storage layer as well. Think of this build habit as vector insurance in case you mess something up. It also lets me easily take elements I may have created for one project and reuse them in another.

2. **Temp**: I use this layer to test things before I actually make them part of the art. The more I build, the more a file can get cluttered visually, so this gives me space to turn off the other layers and work on a clean surface. Once I have the specific vector art dialed in, I move it to the build layer.

3. **Build**: This is where most of my building takes place. It serves as my vector staging ground, where I construct the vector artwork and finesse my Bézier curves.

4. **Sketch**: This is where I place my scanned refined drawing (either a .tif or .psd file with the opacity set to around 20%). I then lock the layer so it cannot move. This image serves as my guide to build from.

Because I do this all the time, I hired a programmer to create a custom script for Illustrator that automatically sets up my document with this layer structure. I've included this script and the simple instructions in the resource files for this book.

As a project progresses from building the base vector graphics and I begin to colorize my design and add in detailing, I continue to add more layers as needed to make managing and editing the artwork easier. I'll cover this in more detail later in the book.

FIELD NOTES

Bézier Curve Jedi Master

Don't be intimidated by the systematic creative process, new methods, or new tools you read about in this book, my Padawan learner. Think of your vector-drawing program as your design lightsaber. Your skill in wielding it will determine how precise your final vector artwork turns out. Let the creative force flow through you. Yes, there is a lot to master. But master you must.

"Try not. Do or do not, there is no try." —Yoda

DESIGN DRILLS:
Deconstructing Design

Not all professional designers and illustrators practice good layer management, but that doesn't mean you shouldn't. In fact, you should, because having an established layer structure for each and every vector art file you create will make the creative process easier to manage.

Organizing and grouping related content on its own layer as you build will let you easily isolate a specific group when edits are needed down the road. And, I assure you, edits will be needed—they always are. Grouping related content by layers lets you to make adjustments faster and refine details in your design without other vector shapes getting in your way.

Let's deconstruct two of my designs. By turning your layers on and off, you'll be able to see how the vector content is organized.

Señor Skully

This design was originally created for a sticker manufacturer, but the client changed directions. So, I turned it into a Day of the Dead poster (**FIGURES 2.29–2.33**).

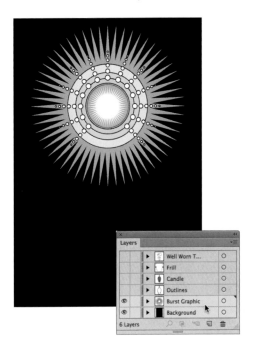

FIGURE 2.29 These two layers make up the background content.

FIGURE 2.30 Keeping my outlines for this design on their own layer makes experimenting with the stroke thickness much easier.

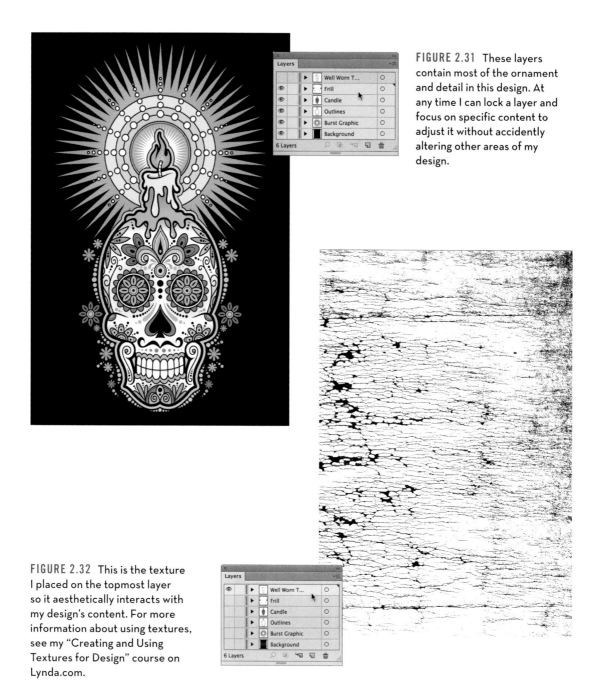

FIGURE 2.31 These layers contain most of the ornament and detail in this design. At any time I can lock a layer and focus on specific content to adjust it without accidently altering other areas of my design.

FIGURE 2.32 This is the texture I placed on the topmost layer so it aesthetically interacts with my design's content. For more information about using textures, see my "Creating and Using Textures for Design" course on Lynda.com.

FIGURE 2.33 Complexity is easily managed with layers in the final Day of the Dead poster design.

Creative Monster

I created this illustration for a poster to promote a creative conference. The detailing is complex, so I used layers to make the creative process easier and more manageable (**FIGURES 2.34–2.38**).

FIGURE 2.34 These five layers make up the base elements of this character illustration. I'll continue to build on these using additional layers.

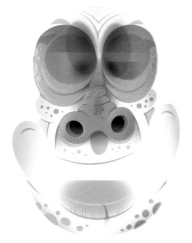

FIGURE 2.35 The hierarchy of layers isn't always in a specific order—you can change it according to the visual needs of your project. The common denominator in these three layers is the use of gradients and blend modes to detail out the design.

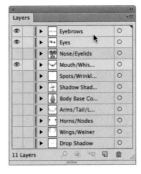

FIGURE 2.36 These three layers contain the facial elements. Because these are complex, I assigned each to its own layer so I could easily access and refine the art.

FIGURE 2.37 With all layers turned on, the character illustration is ready to integrate into the poster layout.

FIGURE 2.38 The final promotional poster shows the creative monster in its final design context. I usually keep my original layered build file separate from my final art file. That way I can always access and reuse it later if needed.

VECTOR
BASIC
TRAINING

CHAPTER 3

Analog Methods in a Digital Age

I, a designer of planet Earth, in order to form a more perfect creative process, establish drawing skills, ensure design tranquility, provide excellent art, promote conceptual welfare, and secure the blessings of creative liberty to ourselves and our posterity, do ordain and establish this chapter for the designers of our world.

Don't Be a Tooler

I graduated from art school in 1986. Even though the program was specifically geared to training graphic designers, we had to take drawing and illustration classes. At the time, our industry realized the importance of drawing as it relates to creative thinking and design.

But times have changed. Most art schools that offer visual communications degrees don't require students to take any drawing classes. The majority of them focus on software-oriented design (a tool-driven process), which only compounds the problem.

This issue isn't limited to recent design school graduates, however. Even seasoned designers who have been trained to draw have sometimes been lulled into creative lethargy by the ease and accessibility of digital tools.

This dumbing down of creativity in our industry is a serious pet peeve of mine. Those who bake down the creative process so it's not too demanding on the individual believe the computer, rather than the artist, is the wellspring of creativity.

The fundamental problem for many designers is the lack of a well-defined and systematic creative process. In today's design reality, it's far too easy to fall into the routine of jumping on the computer as the first step in a creative task. We've all been guilty of this at one time or another. But any designer who jumps directly onto the computer is what I would call a "tooler."

A tooler is someone who doesn't necessarily want to improve his or her drawing skills but thinks that by learning the latest software version, applying a new drop-down menu effect, running a filter in a certain way, or mimicking some other type of convoluted Fibonacci-esque computer-driven function, he or she can avoid drawing.

Toolers don't draw. In making that choice, they not only lessen the quality of the final product but also fail to grow as designers. It's a lose-lose situation.

Analog—that is, drawing—and digital are not independent of each other when it comes to creating artwork. Nothing I do is fully digital, nor is it fully analog. I'm constantly going back and forth between the two throughout the creative process.

I Get Paid to Draw

Early in my career (pre-computer), people would ask me what I did for a living and I'd say, "I'm a graphic designer." The usual response was something like, "You get paid to draw? I can't draw a stick figure." They clearly associated my core skill and craft with what I did for a living.

But now (post-computer) when I tell people what I do, the normal response is something like this: "That's cool. I have a computer, too. I printed some inkjet business cards for..." And they proceed to associate what they do on a PC in their spare time using Microsoft Paint, prefab templates, Comic Sans font, and clip art with what I do as a professional.

Gone is the appreciation or even recognition of a skill or craft we as artists possess to do our jobs. For the most part, toolers don't view themselves as lacking any core ability as "designers" because the computer, in their minds, has replaced the skill and craft they once associated with an artist's ability.

Our industry is inundated with toolers who reinforce this poor public perception of what we do. Toolers don't take skill and craft seriously. In essence, one could argue that they are merely glorified amateurs who just know more about the software than the general public. Mom and Pop see what they produce and say to themselves, "Hey, I can do that, too." And thus the tooler dispensation was born.

As I stated earlier, I don't expect every designer to be a full-blown illustrator—that's simply unrealistic. But I do think every designer should integrate basic drawing skills into the creative process to facilitate his or her full creative potential (**FIGURE 3.1**). This chapter will help you understand the

FIGURE 3.1 Stop basing your design decisions on what you find in drop-down menus and start improving your analog drawing skills.

importance of working out your ideas in analog form before moving to digital—that is, working out your ideas on paper before ever approaching the computer.

Concepts and Ideas

When I teach illustrative design, one of the first things I tell my students is that I can't teach them to be creative. I can only show them methods that will aid them in their quest to create and execute unique concepts and artwork.

Much could be written on the subject of generating ideas and using creative thinking and mental problem solving in a design context. Suffice it to say that this book is intended to facilitate the execution of your ideas—not the creation of them.

A solid creative foundation starts with doing research, knowing your audience, and thinking through ideas that are appropriate for that audience both strategically and aesthetically. Only when these steps are completed can you begin to draw.

Your brain is the only computer you need at this point. You're mining, not refining, so it's important to load the chamber (your brain) with as much relevant information as you can to fuel your creative exploration as you draw out your ideas (**FIGURE 3.2**).

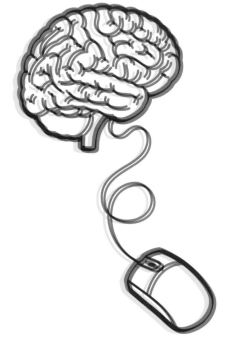

FIGURE 3.2 **You have a supercomputer on your shoulders. Load it with as much information as possible so you can draw on it when needed (pun intended).**

Analog Tools

As I draw out my ideas and work through the creative process, I depend on three tools (**FIGURE 3.3**):

- A 2B pencil for roughing out concepts and chewing on.

- A black Paper Mate Flair pen to quickly create thumbnail sketches.

- A mechanical pencil for drawing refined sketches, which I then scan and build on in my vector drawing program.

I also like to use a black Sharpie and a red pen at times, but those don't play a part in the foundational stage of my creative process. I use them in refining my artwork and in art directing myself, as I'll discuss later.

The Lost Art of Thumbnailing

I love the term "thumbnailing." It's an apropos term to define the capture of ideas in a simple and small drawing. Because you're just mining for concepts at this point, you don't need to worry about how precise or technically accurate the image is. Thumbnails are nothing more than visual triggers to help you explore creative possibilities.

Think of the process as "brain dumping." You're simply opening up the floodgates of your mind and letting the ideas flow out on to paper. Have fun with the process: don't get hung up on how appropriate the concept is at this point or how good the sketches may be. Remember, you're not refining at this point; you're simply mining. You'll go through and refine your direction later.

You could also refer to these as doodles. In reality, the only difference between a traditional doodle and a thumbnail sketch is that one is spontaneous or random and the other tends to be purposeful. But if calling these sketches "doodles" takes the pressure off, then go for it.

An aside: as much as I try to plan for a project, I never know when inspiration will hit me. Many times something I see or think will trigger an

FIGURE 3.3 If the pen is mightier than the sword, then it's a safe bet the mouse is no match for the pen either. So stop whining, grab a pencil, and start drawing.

idea, I'll begin to make mental connections, and I'll grab a pen and paper to sketch some quick thumbnails of the idea so I don't I lose it. This is why you'll see different ink and paper colors in my thumbnail sketches (**FIGURE 3.4**).

Thumbnails may start out very crude, but through a process of refinement they lead to well-crafted and precise digital artwork (**FIGURE 3.5**).

FIGURE 3.4 Thumbnails aplenty. Find the thumbnails that align with the designs on the following page.

FIGURE 3.5 Thumbnailing forms the foundation for any type of creative project, be it pattern design, hand lettering, character design, brand identity, icon design, or a tribal-styled illustration.

More Is Better

You can never have too many thumbnails, but you can have too few. Always push yourself to create more than you need for any given project. This will ensure that you've fully vetted your exploration.

> "Nothing is more dangerous than an idea when it is the only one you have." —ÉMILE CHARTIER

There's a nice fringe benefit to over-thumbnailing: over time, you'll build an archive of "homeless" ideas. When a new project comes along that aligns with a previous project's theme, you can harvest ideas from your unused archive. It's like renewable creative energy!

An Exception to the Rule

There are, of course, exceptions. Not every project needs a lot of thumbnails. Sometimes a design motif is so geometric and simple that you don't need to refine it beyond your initial thumbnail sketch.

Keep your creative process flexible enough to allow this approach without compromising the end results. It obviously won't apply to every job you work on, but in the case of my Freedom of Speech project, it did (**FIGURE 3.6**). The speech bubble element was clearly going to be an easy-to-build object (**FIGURE 3.7**).

I created the motif primarily using basic shapes within my drawing program—why try to draw a perfect elliptical shape when there's already a tool that does it with precision? This applies to the star shape as well.

FIGURE 3.6 My concept was a very graphic and stylized speech bubble that also read as an eagle. This thumbnail gave me enough information to move from analog to digital.

FIGURE 3.7 Final "Freedom of Speech" design—iconic, clean, and impactful.

This project is, of course, the exception, not the rule. More often than not you'll want to thumbnail out your ideas and then redraw and refine your drawn design before trying to pull off the vector artwork.

Refine Your Drawing

Before you get into your car and drive somewhere you've never been before, you probably check a map for directions. If you don't bother reviewing a map, you can easily get lost, drive a route that's out of your way, and experience a lot of frustration as you try to figure things out on the fly.

The same is true when it comes to building vector artwork. Drawing out and refining your ideas gives you a precise road map that you can follow in your vector drawing program. It removes the guesswork from building your art (**FIGURE 3.8**).

But if you don't take the time to think through and draw what you need to build before you build it, you'll waste a lot of time noodling around looking for that result you're after.

FIGURE 3.8 My thumbnail sketch for a character design based on the theme of germs.

Refinement is a process of evolving your art from a rough idea into a clarified plan from which you can build a design. Your goal is the same as an architect's: you draw it the way you plan to build it.

Drawing is an iterative process. So if something just doesn't look right after you've drawn and redrawn it, then it's a good bet you need to keep drawing and rework it even more. Whenever you're in doubt about how your drawing looks, redraw it until you remove that doubt (**FIGURE 3.9**).

FIGURE 3.9 A tighter rough sketch of my original thumbnail.

Refinement isn't a task reserved for just this stage of the creative process; it should blanket the whole process. Over time, you'll learn to art direct yourself and make continual refinements along the way (**FIGURE 3.10**).

FIGURE 3.10 The refined sketch that I used as my road map in my vector drawing program.

I find it a lot easier to draw on vellum and use a light box. I usually redraw only the parts of a drawing that I don't like, and then once I have everything figured out, I just tape them all together to form the final refined sketch that I can scan.

This process takes dedication. If you're not used to working this way, it will seem foreign and laborious, and I can almost guarantee that you'll get frustrated. But anything worth doing is always hard at first, so hang in there. It will get easier, and you'll get better at it.

You may invest more time at the beginning of a project, but it will save you time later when you actually start creating the art. It'll also expand your creative skill set, hone your craftsmanship, and equip you to produce better work.

Create a Better Road Map

Have you ever tried to follow a map that wasn't accurate? It kind of defeats the purpose. The same is true when you draw out your refined artwork. The more precise it is, the easier it will be to build it in vector form. Once you're happy with your drawing, you can scan it in and place it into your vector drawing program.

The following project demonstrates how drawing serves as an accurate road map for building your art (**FIGURES 3.11–3.14**). The initial thumbnail, rough sketch, and final refined sketch are shown on the previous two pages.

FIGURE 3.11 This tighter sketch was closer to what I needed but still too rough to build from. It would have taken more time to finesse the vectors than to just redraw it in a more final form before moving to digital.

FIGURE 3.12 I removed all of the guesswork by building on top of a refined drawing. This gave me a clear road map of where to place my anchor points and how my vector paths should be shaped.

FIGURE 3.13 The refined sketch let me build my base vector artwork with precision.

FIGURE 3.14 The final vector artwork of my germ character design.

This sketch-and-refine process can apply to any type of design project that needs to end up in vector form. This example showcases a custom hand-lettered logotype design (**FIGURES 3.15–3.21**).

FIGURE 3.15 This thumbnail sketch established the general composition and direction for my hand-lettered design.

FIGURE 3.16 In this tighter sketch, I continued to refine my artwork. At this point I wasn't worrying about precise shapes, just trying to flesh out the look and feel and balance the weight of the letterforms and negative space.

FIGURE 3.17 I started drawing my refined sketch on my light box with my rough sketch underneath. I was thinking about vector shapes. How would I go about building this in vector form? Drawing my art precisely in analog facilitated how I would build it in digital.

FIGURE 3.18 The refined sketch, ready to scan and place into my drawing program.

FIGURE 3.19 The refined sketch that I used as a road map to build my vector shapes with precision. At this point, I wasn't guessing how I'd form them; I just followed what I determined in the drawing stage.

FIGURE 3.20 Once I selected my color palette for the design, I decided to work in some subtle texturing to give it an organic flair.

FIGURE 3.21 The final hand-lettered design. Yes, that's me and one of my favorite sayings: "Full Tilt Creative Boogie!"

Back and Forth

 Here's another real-world project that illustrates why the analog-to-vector process is essential. For this project I had to illustrate a three-eyed monster in a pseudo-woodcut style. To pull this off, I had to go back and forth between analog and digital throughout its creation (**FIGURES 3.22–3.30**).

FIGURE 3.22 Thumbnail sketch for "Tri3ye Guy" illustration.

FIGURE 3.23 An illustration like this doesn't go fast. And I make sure to scrutinize each and every shape I draw.

FIGURE 3.24 My refined sketch, ready to scan in. Since the illustration was symmetrical, I only had to draw out half of it in Illustrator. (You'll learn more about symmetry in the "Symmetry Is Your Friend" section of Chapter 6, "Vector Build Methods.")

FIGURE 3.25 No guesswork was needed to build vector shapes. I simply followed what I'd already predetermined in my refined sketch.

FIGURE 3.26 I built my base black-and-white vector art and then printed it out and drew on it to get the shading I wanted. During a project like this, I go from digital back to analog several times to work out all of the detail in my illustration.

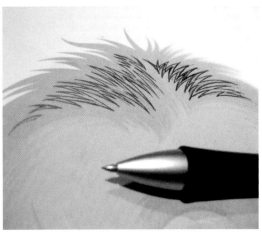

FIGURE 3.27 A refined drawing of highlight detail in the figure's hair. I could have tried to render this without drawing it first, but it would have taken me a lot longer and probably not looked as good.

FIGURE 3.28 Using vellum, I drew on top of a color printout using my light box to work out highlight details that I'd need to build out in vector form. This process of going back and forth from digital to analog eventually becomes second nature.

FIGURE 3.29 This image shows a close-up of the shading and highlight detailing in this illustration.

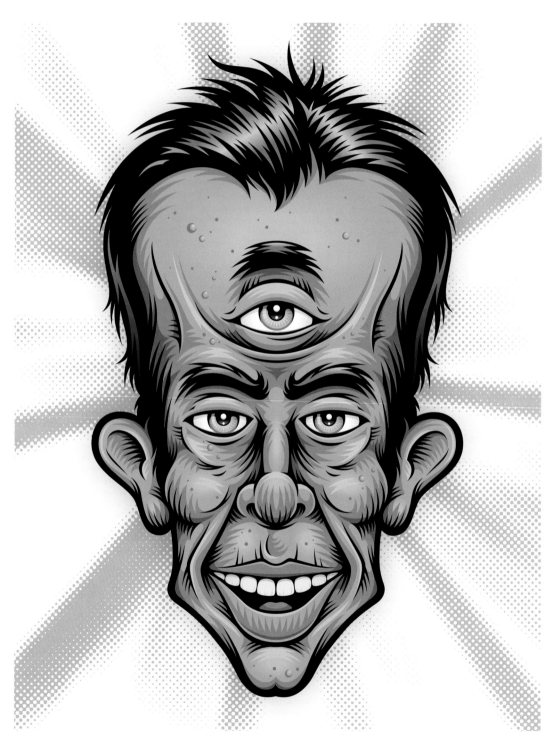

FIGURE 3.30 Final "Tri3ye Guy" illustration. He's a looker.

Systematic and Creative

Most of the time we create on behalf of our clients. Our design solutions need to work professionally within a commercial environment. And our creative work has to fit with a client's business personality and marketing strategy. We also need to create artwork within a set budget and schedule, which means we don't have the luxury of spending as much time as we might like on any given project.

These are all reasons why a systematic creative process is necessary when creating vector-based artwork. Building your vector designs on a solid creative foundation is a must in order to produce work that's precise, on time, and effective.

The more you work systematically as you build vector artwork, the more the process becomes second nature, and the faster you'll be able to execute your ideas without compromising the quality of the art.

Let's take a look at this systematic process in context of a more complex project: a visual identity for a clothing company called Beloved Virus (**FIGURES 3.31–3.43**).

FIGURE 3.31 Part of developing a visual identity for this client was developing initial concepts for a new business name. Once we had the name nailed down, I began fleshing out a wide assortment of thumbnail sketches to determine the various directions I'd take. Drawing isn't merely a skill for visual design; it's a great way to enhance thinking as well.

FIGURE 3.32 I wanted the mark to be more timeless and less gimmicky, so I liked the idea of an ornate, hand-lettered typographic treatment. At this stage, I put meat on the bones of my idea and started defining the design. This gave me a good idea of what to expect, but it still wasn't good enough to build from.

FIGURE 3.33 I redrew the letterforms more precisely with my mechanical pencil. Here I was still scrutinizing the balance of the shapes and looking for areas I could refine and improve further.

FIGURE 3.34 I put the project aside for the day and approached it with fresh eyes the next morning. This helped me isolate problem areas and fix them before I went to digital. I modified several letterforms and was ready to create my refined sketch.

FIGURE 3.35 On this project, I scanned in and printed out my rough at a larger size so I could redraw the refined sketch with maximum precision.

FIGURE 3.36 I scanned my refined sketch and now had an exact road map from which to build my vector artwork on. No guesswork was involved; I already knew what the logo should look like.

FIGURE 3.37 Whenever I build vector artwork, I form my art by creating smaller shapes. It's far easier than trying to create using one single shape. (Note: This and all of the build techniques demonstrated in this chapter will be explained in upcoming chapters.)

FIGURE 3.38 For example, look at the letter *B*. It's made from eight different individual shapes. If I tried to build this as one or two shapes, it would be a major pain to get it built precisely. The end result wouldn't be as elegant either.

FIGURE 3.39 I continued using this same build method to create all of the letterforms for this design. Ironically, the process looks sloppy, but it produces precise results.

FIGURE 3.40 I call this simple method "shape building." (You'll learn more about this in Chapter 6.)

FIGURE 3.41 I fused all of the shapes together to form the base art for the brand logo.

FIGURE 3.42 Along the way, I distorted the perspective of the type treatment and contained it within a dimensional nesting shape to give it more volume. The end result was an effective, precision-built brand logotype derived from the solid creative foundation of drawing.

FIGURE 3.43 I used the same systematic process to design and build all of the logo concepts I presented to my client.

If you've determined that you can't do the drawing part of this process very well, then my book has taught you something already: you need to improve your core drawing skills. That's what growing as a designer is all about.

I'm often asked, "How do I get better at drawing?" There's no secret, the answer is easy: you just start, and you stick with it. If you start drawing today (doodling counts, by the way), in five years you'll be a lot better at it.

One of the coolest aspects of a creative career is that talent and skill don't diminish over time. Like wine, they only get better with age. But if you never start, you'll never improve, and you'll miss out on creative opportunities.

The whole reason for drawing out your vector art before you build it is to create a piece of digital art that is precise and well-crafted. Your final art will just come out better.

When Is a Drawing Done?

You draw out your thumbnail sketches, isolate a good idea, rough it out, redraw it, and refine it multiple times. It begs the question:

"How do I know when I'm done drawing?"

The answer depends on the person who's doing the drawing. If the drawing doesn't feel right, then you know you're not done refining it. When I say "feel," I mean it literally. It's a second-sense type of thing. You just get to a point where you know it looks right.

If something is bugging you about your drawing, then it's a good bet you need to redraw something. Stepping away from your project and approaching it later with fresh eyes will help you see where you can make improvements.

I'll cover this in more depth in Chapter 8, "Art Directing Yourself."

But if that isn't enough, vector artwork is resolution independent, which means that you can use it in almost any format or application. It extends your design's creative possibilities.

I've shown you the importance of drawing out your ideas and refining them, but you've seen only a glimpse of the actual vector build methods you'll use in your vector drawing program once your drawing is complete.

You may be saying to yourself at this point, "I can draw out my ideas, but actually building the vector art is a major pain in the ass."

Fear not, my weary friend! The next three chapters will demystify vector building through simple, systematic methods that will equip you for success.

DESIGN DRILLS:
Essential Nonsense

I'd never say that I completely understand all of my own doodles, because I don't. Most just flow out of me without any forethought. I simply open up the floodgates and see what happens. It's more fun that way.

I'll admit that most are strange, and some are a bit disturbing. The latter category I refer to as "Dark Morsels." Once again, don't ask me what they mean.

That said, I think doodling is a great way to exercise creativity. That's why I consider doodling *essential nonsense*. The following examples showcase a rogue's gallery of bizarre doodles harvested from the deepest recesses of my mind (**FIGURES 3.44–3.51**).

I've also included a project walk-through where I show how I narrowed down a collection of doodles and thumbnail sketches into a rather hairy self-promotional piece (**FIGURES 3.52–3.56**).

Doodling also lends itself to practical purposes on real world projects like the editorial illustration shown in Chapter 10, "Good Creative Habits," Figure 10.1.

FIGURE 3.44 Meet Mr. Crusty Pants. He loves spinning a good conspiracy yarn.

FIGURE 3.45 A prophetic look at social media in the year 2028: aged Twitter acolytes genetically modify themselves with bird DNA, while slinging verbal arrows and smoking government-approved big pharma.

FIGURE 3.46 A watcher.

FIGURE 3.47 Hurry up and formulate your persona.

FIGURE 3.48 Pac-Man has fallen on hard times. He also likes to swear in Klingon.

FIGURE 3.49 Sometimes current events inspire my doodles, like this incarnation of H1N1.

FIGURE 3.50 "Hacking Reality," which apparently involves the consumption of fish water.

FIGURE 3.51 "Really Weird," a screen-printed promotional poster for Neenah Paper.

FIGURE 3.52 Sometimes the best marketing ideas leverage pop culture. I decided to create a fun and interactive marketing piece that also promoted my illustration work. These are thumbnail sketches for an illustrative mask inspired by the popularity of beards and by Twitter.

FIGURE 3.54 My refined sketch of my mask artwork I'll now scan in and build from.

FIGURE 3.53 More thumbnail sketches and the isolation of the idea I'll move forward with.

FIGURE 3.55 No guesswork vector building using the refined sketch as my guide.

FIGURE 3.56 My final illustrative mask, Twitter Beard. My snarky daughter Savannah demonstrates its use.

VECTOR
BASIC
TRAINING

CHAPTER 4

Getting to the Points

A Bézier curve or path is only as elegant, graceful, or accurate as the anchor points that control and shape it. To better control and edit anchor points, you first need to understand and recognize what qualifies as a good anchor point and path, a bad anchor point and path, and an ugly anchor point and path.

A vector design can easily have hundreds of paths and thousands of anchor points within it. Each point that's incorrectly used or sloppily handled will just add to the overall degradation of your visual aesthetic.

Anyone can learn to use a digital tool; that's merely a skill set. I want you to become a vector craftsman, someone who can handle the basic tools and create professional results. You may conceive of a brilliant idea, but if your vector craftsmanship is weak, it doesn't matter how well thought out the idea is. It will suffer from poor execution when you build the vector artwork.

On Prime Point Placement

There's one key question to ask before you can determine whether an anchor point is good, bad, or ugly: is it in the correct position within your design? That is, is the Prime Point Placement (PPP) of your anchor point correct? Chapter 5, "Shape Surveillance," covers placing and removing anchor points, as well as PPP, in more detail. But suffice it to say for now that if an anchor point isn't positioned ideally as you build your vector shape, it will make controlling the path so that it matches your drawing far more difficult and possibly inaccurate.

For the sake of demonstration, all the vector art in **FIGURES 4.1–4.3** contains identical PPP. That is, the anchor points are in the ideal locations. The only difference among the figures is in the specific problematic characteristics associated with the individual anchor points themselves.

With that graphic caveat in mind, let's take a closer look.

The Good Anchor Point and Path

To demonstrate the good, the bad, and the ugly as those qualities apply to anchor points and paths, I've selected an ornament design that contains only one straight line and depends mainly on the use of Bézier curves to form its overall shape.

First, however, it's important to understand the difference between corner anchor points and smooth anchor points. A *corner* anchor point is placed anywhere there's an apex that comes to a point. It can be used with or without Bézier curve handles pulled out from one or both sides when the transition between two paths doesn't need to be smooth or continuous.

A *smooth* anchor point is placed anywhere there's a curve that transitions elegantly from one path into the next smoothly. This sort of anchor point *always* uses Bézier curve handles pulled out from both sides to control the shape of the curved path.

The anchor points controlling the Bézier curves that form the main vine in the motif shown in **FIGURE 4.1** bend smoothly from one side to the other, creating graceful curves.

The handles are parallel with one another and aren't pulled out too far, ensuring smooth continuity throughout the art. The other anchor point handles that form the remaining Bézier curves are also not overextended; they are pulled out only as far as needed to form each of the various bends in the path.

The end result of good anchor points and paths is elegant final artwork.

FIGURE 4.1 Elegant results come from correct use of corner and smooth anchor points and handles. The anchor point positions and the paths they create are on the left; the resulting final shape is on the right.

The Bad Anchor Point and Path

In the vector ornament design shown in **FIGURE 4.2**, the anchor points are the correct type, but their handles are used incorrectly. They're not parallel with one another, so the Bézier curves look less elegant, and the visual continuity of the overall path is lost. A consistent creative process that utilizes PPP and The Clockwork Method (introduced in Chapter 5) will help you steer clear of this problem. At this point, the goal is simply to recognize that something is definitely not right. The end result of bad anchor points and paths is a less graceful form, and thus the final art is more clunky.

FIGURE 4.2 The anchor points in this vector ornament design are the correct type; the problem lies with their handles. Again, the anchor point positions and paths are on the left, and the resulting shape is on the right.

The Ugly Anchor Point and Path

Almost all the anchor points in **FIGURE 4.3** are the incorrect type. For any Bézier curve that you want to transition smoothly from one side of an anchor point to the opposite side, use a smooth anchor point, not a corner anchor point. Using the wrong type of anchor point will cause a curved shape to look pointed, as shown in the top arch of the vine.

More problems: Many of the anchor point handles aren't parallel with one another, and some are pulled out too far, which prevents continuous flow through the art and makes parts of it look flat. Some of the other anchor point handles that form the remaining Bézier curves in the design are overextended as well.

FIGURE 4.3 This is what happens when anchor points are the wrong type. As usual, the anchor point positions and paths are on the left, and the resulting less-than-ideal shape is on the right.

FIGURE 4.4 The finished design has a total of 18 closed paths and 340 anchor points.

Some of these problems emerge from sloppy building habits, such as not zooming in when you build, which can result in anchor points being placed in positions that aren't going to work well. It all comes down to proper craftsmanship and paying attention to detail. **FIGURE 4.4** shows the final context for this artwork.

A Scrutinizing Eye

You'll need to pay close attention to your anchor points and paths throughout the vector build process to ensure that you're creating quality. That said, no one is perfect; you'll make mistakes as you create your vector art, so it's important to train yourself to spot potential problems as you review.

It may seem like I'm asking you to micromanage your vector art, and in part that's true. But over time it will become second nature, to the point that you won't even consciously think about which anchor points to place or handles to pull. You will, however, notice the steady improvement in your vector shapes because of your due diligence.

The Vector No-Fly List

Be on the lookout for the following common vector building mistakes:

- **Incorrect anchor point:** If you're creating a Bézier curve that bends smoothly from one side of an anchor point into the opposite side, as shown in **FIGURE 4.5**, use a smooth anchor point rather than a corner anchor point. If the curve looks pointed, then you're using an incorrect anchor point in the path.

  To convert a corner anchor point to a smooth anchor point (and vice versa), select the problem anchor point and click the "Convert selected anchor points to smooth" button in the Control panel (Figure 4.5). The opposite option will appear if the point is already smooth. (Unfortunately, there's no keyboard command for this, nor is it recordable via actions.)

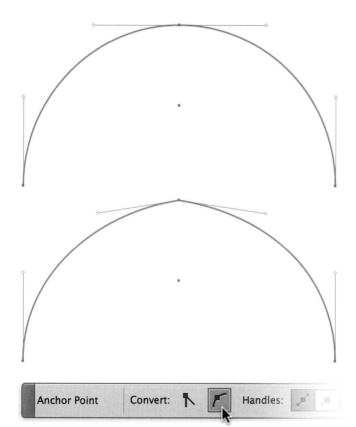

FIGURE 4.5 The correct use of a smooth anchor point (top) and an incorrect corner anchor point, which causes a pointed look (bottom). In a design that contains thousands of anchor points, it's important to scrutinize as you build or you can easily overlook a problematic anchor point.

FIGURE 4.6 Properly extended anchor point handles (top) and a curve with overextended anchor point handles, which cause a flat appearance (bottom).

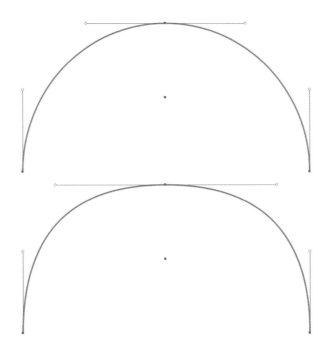

- **Flat curves:** If you pull out your anchor point handles too far on a Bézier curve that bends smoothly from one side of an anchor point to the opposite side (**FIGURE 4.6**), the curve will lose its roundness and begin to appear flat. Flatness in a curve is a telltale sign of overextended handles.

- **Parallels:** When you create shapes that contain corresponding Bézier curves that bend smoothly from one side of an anchor point to the opposite side (**FIGURE 4.7**), make sure the extended handles at the apex of the curve are parallel with one another. If the end vector shape doesn't have a graceful flow, it's a good bet some of the handles aren't parallel.

- **Overextended handles:** This is the result of trying to span the distance between two anchor points using one anchor point handle instead of both. Much like the flat curve problem, it will result in a shape that is flat, awkward, and clunky. It also can cause mitering problems on severe angles, if you use a heavier stroke (**FIGURE 4.8**).

FIGURE 4.7 Parallel handles shown (top) and nonparallel handles, which cause an uneven result (bottom). This won't apply to every arch, but it will apply to most curved vector shapes.

FIGURE 4.8 Both handles of each path properly pulled out to form Bézier curves (top); trying to achieve the same curve using only one overextended handle causes flatness, resulting in a clunky shape and mitering problems (bottom).

A Good Example

It's good to have a critical eye as you build your vector work to ensure that you're avoiding the telltale signs of problematic anchor points and the Bézier curves they control.

But it's even more important to recognize good anchor point characteristics. As your eye develops, you'll be able to look at any vector graphic and pinpoint the good or bad characteristics of its anchor points and curves.

FIGURE 4.9 This complex vector ornament design contains no straight lines whatsoever. It depends on precisely built Bézier curves created from smooth and corner anchor points. You won't find any of the "no-fly list" problems in this motif.

I should point out that the design shown in **FIGURES 4.9** and **4.10** took me about eight hours to build. I had to rebuild several shapes a few times before I dialed in the vector art precisely. I mention this because it would be easy for me to say that if you follow my process, everything will be easy and work the first time. That isn't true.

FIGURE 4.10 Final vector artwork for a die-hard Mac fanboy who loves his Apple iPad so much that he hired me to design this custom ornament, which he'll get etched into the back of the device.

Change Your Perspective

When scrutinizing your vector shapes, it's a good idea to select and rotate or flip them, print them out larger, or change your view to outline in Adobe Illustrator to help pinpoint areas you can improve on. If you don't do this, your eyes can easily get used to what they're looking at, which makes it harder to see problems.

Changing the visual perspective and orientation of the art forces your mind to reassess the shapes and determine whether something needs to be fixed or just doesn't look right. It's the same principle as holding a drawing up to a mirror in order to discover a distortion.

You'll learn more about self-art direction in Chapter 8, "Art Directing Yourself."

What is true about my process is that it's a *process*. Part of that process is recognizing the good and bad characteristics in your own art and in the art of others. While creating this design, I had to remind myself of The Clockwork Method. I wasn't following it, and my shapes were looking wonky.

Thank Goodness for Command-Z/Control-Z

Even with this systematic approach to building vector graphics, not every piece of vector artwork you create will be perfect. I still make mistakes every day. Placing anchor points and manipulating handles takes some trial and error.

The ultimate goals of this book are to dramatically reduce your potential for making mistakes, to help you to recognize when something isn't right, and to show you how to fix problems quickly so you can continue building your designs. So when in doubt, Command-Z (or Control-Z) can be your best form of creative accountability.

Remember, the creative process is almost always a messy one. Don't focus on perfection. Focus on your process, because process makes perfect.

DESIGN DRILLS:
Vector Skeletons

Proper anchor point placement is critical for creating precise vector artwork. But, unless you have your vector paths selected (V), it can be difficult to tell where all the anchor points reside within a given path.

FIGURES 4.11–4.14 show the vector skeletons for two very different sorts of design projects so you can see exactly where the anchor points are placed and how those placements affect the final artwork.

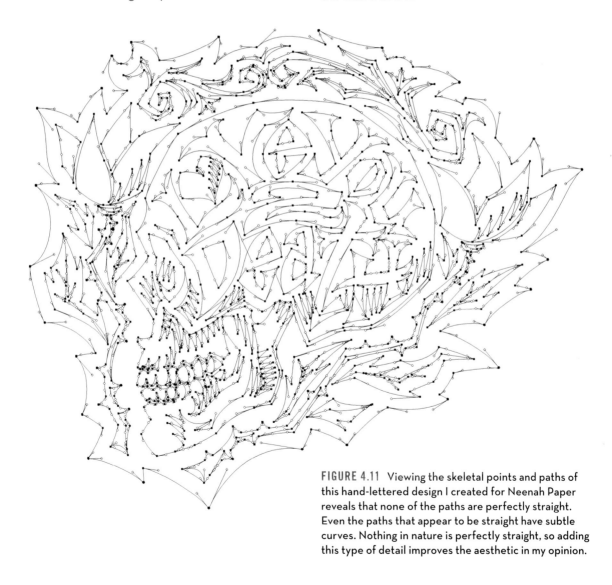

FIGURE 4.11 Viewing the skeletal points and paths of this hand-lettered design I created for Neenah Paper reveals that none of the paths are perfectly straight. Even the paths that appear to be straight have subtle curves. Nothing in nature is perfectly straight, so adding this type of detail improves the aesthetic in my opinion.

FIGURE 4.12 Placed bitmap textures give the final poster design a more organic look and feel. For more information regarding the use of textures in your designs, see DrawingVectorGraphics.com.

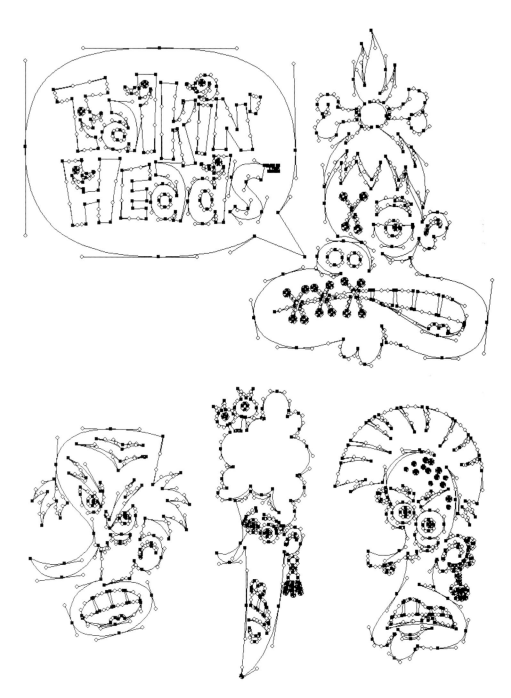

FIGURE 4.13 Not all art requires a massive number of anchor points. I used only seven anchor points to form the speech bubble in this logotype design for a stock illustration set.

FIGURE 4.14 This final art shows four of the 50 "talkin' heads" I created for this stock illustration set.

CHAPTER 5

Shape Surveillance

It's time to take your refined drawing out of analog and move it into the digital realm. To do this accurately, you need to place your anchor points precisely so they form the paths needed to create your final vector art.

It does no good to spend time up front drawing and refining your shapes on paper only to fall short by building them poorly onscreen. Placing points incorrectly wastes time in the build stage of your creative process and, ultimately, gives you imprecise vector results.

I can't stress enough the importance of proper anchor point placement. You must be able to look at any visual shape, drawn or otherwise, and know exactly how to go about building it, anchor point by anchor point. This chapter will show you how to start the build process. Chapter 6, "Vector Build Methods," will show you how to accurately finish the build.

The Clockwork Method

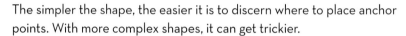

The simpler the shape, the easier it is to discern where to place anchor points. With more complex shapes, it can get trickier.

To help you in your shape study, I've created The Clockwork Method (TCM). It's a simple way to look at any shape and determine precisely where to place points. Basically, you imagine the clock face in your mind, rotate it as needed to orient with the shapes in your art, and use it as a guide.

When you first learned how to use a vector program like Adobe Illustrator, you most likely figured out on your own where to place anchor points when building vector shapes. You probably focused more on the tools that you needed to create vector graphics and less on the creative process that utilizes the tools.

Over time and through trial and error, you no doubt developed your skills enough to make the program work for your needs. You might still struggle, though, to pull off well-crafted vector shapes. The source of that struggle can be blamed on not knowing exactly where to place the anchor points that make up the design you want to create.

I know this was true for me. And it was only when I started teaching advanced digital illustration at a local college that I developed a coherent method that I could relay to my students and demystify the process of anchor point placement. The Clockwork Method circumvents the hassle of figuring everything out piecemeal over a period of years.

A circle provides the simplest illustration of TCM. The circle would receive anchor points at the 12-, 3-, 6-, and 9-o'clock positions (**FIGURE 5.1**). More complex shapes that contain both concave and convex curves won't necessarily receive all four points every time, as you'll see.

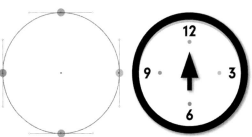

For shapes that are not straight up and down, you can also tilt the clock face so it better corresponds with that shape. **FIGURE 5.2** shows how the tilt works and how easily it adapts to the situation and your preference in regard to anchor point placement. The 9 o'clock anchor point (highlighted blue on the left) could just as well be discerned by someone else as a 12 o'clock (highlighted green on the right) by rotating the clock in his or her mind 90 degrees instead. The Prime Point Placement (PPP) on both is still correct using TCM. (More on PPP in a bit.) It all depends on how you see it in your mind.

FIGURE 5.1 The vector circle shape at left corresponds to the clock positions on the right. I've used four different colors on the TCM clock as well as on the circle art so that you can see the correspondence here and in upcoming illustrations.

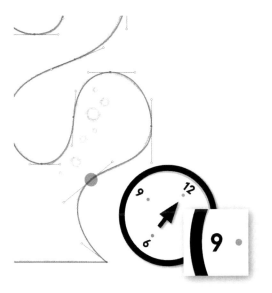
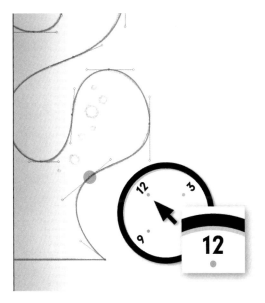

FIGURE 5.2 In this example, the 12 o'clock position is shown in two different orientations. Both are correct. Every person sees the clock orientation in his or her mind differently, but the end result is that both orientations match the curves in the art.

As Figure 5.2 suggests, your art is bound to contain many shapes, perhaps hundreds. Each individual curve that makes up the overall shape of your art will have its own custom-angled clock face.

It's just that simple and just that flexible. Look at every shape you need to build in vector form through the transparent clock face of TCM. It will help remove the guesswork when you place your anchor points.

Train Your Brain

This method may feel a bit strange at first, but using TCM is nothing more than a mental trick to help you look at any form, isolate the various shapes (or curves) that are in it, and associate them with a clock orientation in your mind to discern the anchor point placements.

Let's start by isolating shapes. In **FIGURE 5.3** and **FIGURE 5.4**, you can see how I isolate particular areas of my art. Some curves define interior shapes, while some define exterior shapes. Once I've identified visual associations with these shapes using TCM, I can properly discern the placement of the anchor points, as shown in Figure 5.4.

FIGURE 5.5 provides a more challenging design for your TCM consideration. The shapes are freeform and might require you to mentally rotate and orient your clock to match its curves.

As you did in Figures 5.3 and 5.4, begin to associate your mental clock with the shapes in the drawn form. Remember that when you make these visual associations, you may not use all four points on the clock to form the needed shape. In Figure 5.4, you'll notice that many of the anchor point placements on the left side required only one point of association with the clock to form the needed curve.

FIGURE 5.6 shows how I see the first clock orientation in my mind. Continue your shape surveillance by studying the drawn art and using TCM to discern where the anchor points would be placed according to the clock in your own mind. Compare with **FIGURE 5.7** and see how well you did.

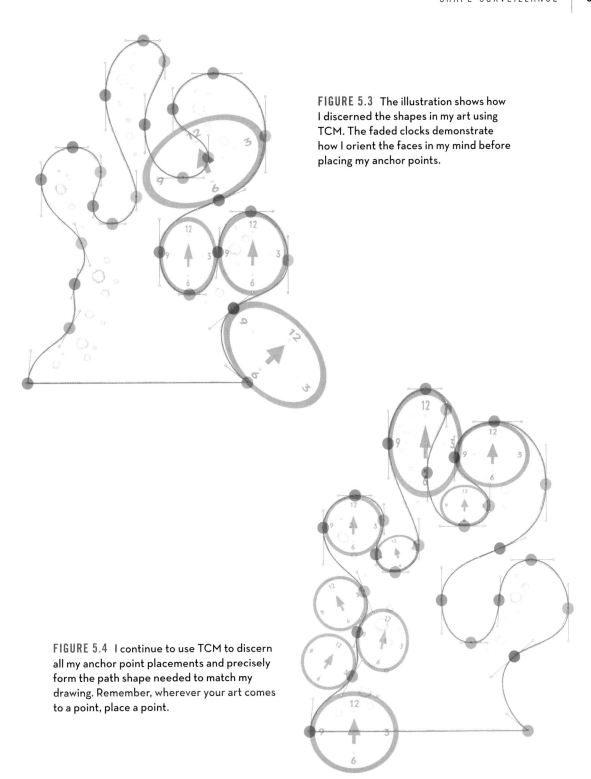

FIGURE 5.3 The illustration shows how I discerned the shapes in my art using TCM. The faded clocks demonstrate how I orient the faces in my mind before placing my anchor points.

FIGURE 5.4 I continue to use TCM to discern all my anchor point placements and precisely form the path shape needed to match my drawing. Remember, wherever your art comes to a point, place a point.

FIGURE 5.5 Look at this drawn shape and decide where you'd place anchor points using TCM. You may not need to use all four clock points on every curved shape.

FIGURE 5.6 Using TCM, I've discerned the first shape in the form. Can you discern where the rest of the anchor points would be placed? Refer to Figures 5.3 and 5.4 for help if you need it.

FIGURE 5.7 This shows the final TCM locations of the anchor points. How did your discernment of the drawing in Figure 5.6 compare to this?

You'll build your vector art one anchor point at a time, mentally picturing the clock, rotating it if needed, and associating the point on the clock with the anchor point you need to place to form the specific curve within the drawn form. Some curved shapes may associate with one or more points of the clock; it all depends on how you visualize it in your mind. Once you've discerned an anchor point's location, place it and then move to the next shape in your design. Repeat the same process until you have the entire vector path built (**FIGURE 5.8**).

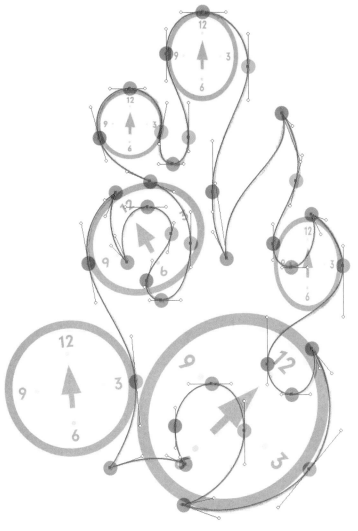

FIGURE 5.8 This shows many of the mental TCM discernments made to determine the final PPP.

Applying TCM

Of course, all shapes aren't as simple as the circle shown in Figure 5.1. Art usually contains many different shapes and curves with many different angles. Still, discerning the anchor point placement on any shape is easier if you use TCM. Regardless of how irregular a shape may be, if you think of it as a clock, you'll be able to place the anchor points with greater accuracy.

Let's try TCM on another shape. Remember, the first step is to analyze the curves in the art (**FIGURE 5.9**). Then, think of the clock positions and you can roughly approximate them on those shapes. (Again, refer to Figures 5.3 and 5.4.) Because of the angles in the shapes of this flame motif, rotate your mental clock to associate it with the many curves within the art.

Where do you start? The most obvious anchor point placements within any design are the areas that come to a point. Those are no-brainers, and it's a good place to start your building because you don't have to discern anything. These are absolutes: any area of your art that comes to a point gets a point (**FIGURE 5.10**).

After you've identified all the angles that come to a point, you can move on to determine the other coordinates (**FIGURES 5.11–5.13**).

The more you train your brain to discern shapes using TCM, the easier it gets. Like anything new, it feels awkward and strange at first, but stick with it and you'll enjoy the results.

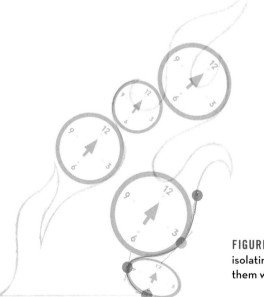

FIGURE 5.9 The first step is to perform shape surveillance by isolating the various curved shapes and mentally associating them with a clock.

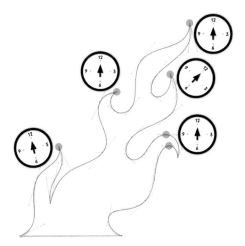

FIGURE 5.10 Most of the anchor points in this design are corner anchor points since shapes in the artwork come to a point. These are the easiest to discern because any art that comes to a point gets a point. Other easy-to-discern anchor points in this motif associate with a mental clock orientation of 12 o'clock.

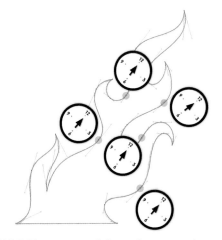

FIGURE 5.11 Here are all the anchor points that match the 3 o'clock orientation.

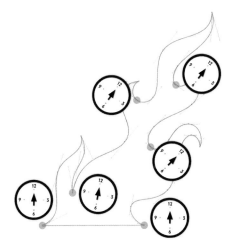

FIGURE 5.12 Here are all the anchor points that match the 6 o'clock orientation. Even though you know that all art that comes to a point gets a point, I'm showing you how the clock can still associate with those locations as well.

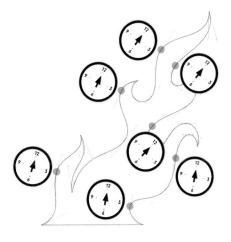

FIGURE 5.13 Here are all the anchor points that match the 9 o'clock orientation.

Many variables will affect the quality of your vector art, as discussed in previous chapters. But determining your anchor point locations is a fundamental aspect of building your vector graphics. Get the anchor point locations wrong, and you'll have a hard time building.

You'll learn more about Prime Point Placement later in this chapter.

More on Rotating Your Clock

As I mentioned before, when a shape within your design is angled, it helps to angle your clock face to match it. Since this can be more confusing than a simple north/south orientation, let's consider another example.

In **FIGURE 5.14**, many of the anchor points run along angled paths. In such cases, simply set your mental clock face to the same angle and start placing points. This is an instance for which one clock face can accommodate all of the angles. (You could also select the vector art and your placed refined sketch and rotate them to align with a normal north/south TCM orientation. I've done that on occasion, but it isn't always practical.)

FIGURE 5.14 If a shape requires a path that needs an anchor point that falls outside the normal orientation of TCM, rotate the TCM clock to match the angle of your artwork.

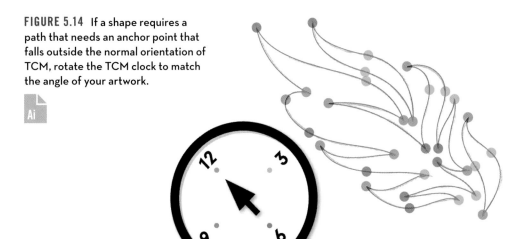

SHAPE SURVEILLANCE | **99**

Most of your designs will require you to rotate the TCM orientation to determine your anchor point placements, so that should be expected.

Building Complex Shapes

To demonstrate TCM on an even more complex shape, let's look at the elegant ornament design in **FIGURE 5.15**. The shapes in this art demand precise Bézier curves that can be achieved only if the anchor points are in the correct locations.

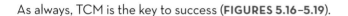

As always, TCM is the key to success (**FIGURES 5.16–5.19**).

FIGURE 5.15 Using TCM, I'll begin to perform shape surveillance on my refined sketch to figure out where to place the initial anchor points. The obvious locations are the pointed tips found throughout the vine. Once again, wherever your art comes to a point gets a point.

FIGURE 5.16 Using my refined sketch as my road map, I place my initial anchor points using TCM. At this stage, the correspondence between the drawn lines and the sketch lines underneath isn't perfect. I call this stage of the process a rough build. That said, my anchor points are in just the right spot. This will let me easily adjust the handles and push and pull the paths to form this graphic motif.

FIGURE 5.17 Once my anchor points are located in their correct positions, it's simply a matter of pulling out my Bézier curve handles to shape the paths so they match my refined drawing and create the intended form.

FIGURE 5.18 I continue to utilize TCM to build all the individual shapes that make up this ornament design (points and handles are not displayed in this image). Notice how my overall motif is created from numerous shapes. (Shape building is covered in greater detail in Chapter 6.)

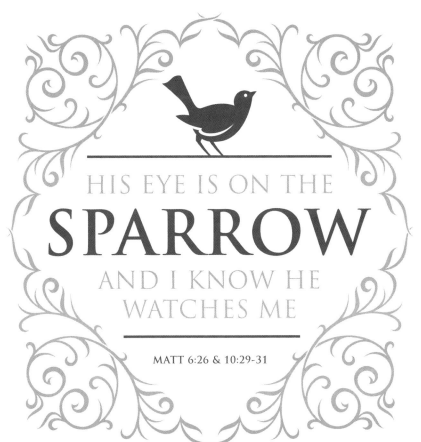

HIS EYE IS ON THE

SPARROW

AND I KNOW HE
WATCHES ME

MATT 6:26 & 10:29-31

FIGURE 5.19 The final vector artwork in context.

Prime Point Placement

At the risk of sounding redundant, not to mention redundant, this bears repeating: When it comes to building your design using vector methods, it's of paramount importance that the initial anchor points you place are in the best possible locations as they relate to the shape you're attempting to form.

The paths in your final vector shape and the Bézier curves they utilize will be only as precise as the anchor points that control them. Make sure that the Prime Point Placement of your anchor points is correct.

TCM will get you in the right neighborhood, but PPP will pinpoint the exact address at which your anchor point will live. Determining the exact location is a process, not an event, so you'll be leveraging both methods to fine-tune your anchor point locations.

Making a Point!

In the previous chapter, you learned about the two types of anchor points: corner and smooth. Knowing how each controls a Bézier curve and path will help you understand where to place them using both TCM and PPP.

- **Corner anchor point:** Place a corner anchor point anywhere your art has an apex that comes to a point. You can use these types of anchor points with or without Bézier curve handles pulled out from one or both sides when the transition between two path segments doesn't need to be smooth (**FIGURE 5.20**).

- **Smooth anchor point:** Place a smooth anchor point anywhere your art needs a curve that transitions from one path segment into the next. This sort of anchor point *always* uses Bézier curve handles pulled out from both sides to control the shape of the curved path (**FIGURE 5.21**).

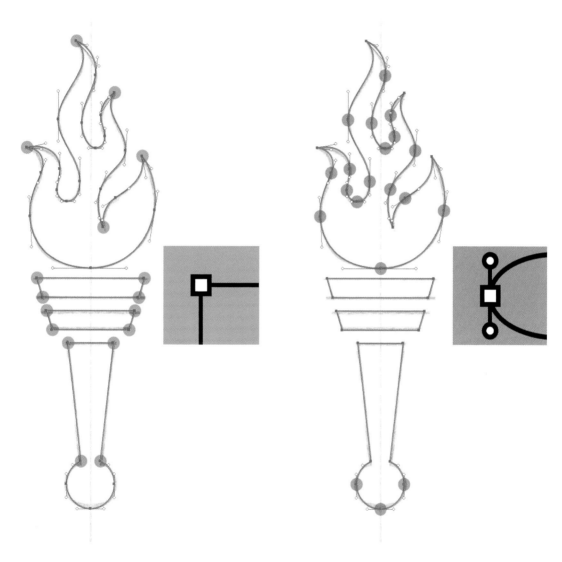

FIGURE 5.20 There are 17 corner anchor points in the build shapes of this torch graphic (highlighted in orange). The handle of the torch is made almost entirely from corner anchor points.

FIGURE 5.21 There are 20 smooth anchor points in the build shapes of this torch graphic (highlighted in purple). The flame contains numerous Bézier curves, so most of the anchor points to shape it are smooth.

Combining PPP and TCM

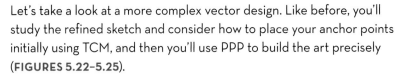

Let's take a look at a more complex vector design. Like before, you'll study the refined sketch and consider how to place your anchor points initially using TCM, and then you'll use PPP to build the art precisely (**FIGURES 5.22–5.25**).

Note that the final design for this example (**FIGURE 5.25**) is symmetrical, so you have to build only half of it—you can copy the final paths and flip them to form the final art. (Chapter 6 covers more benefits of symmetrical design.)

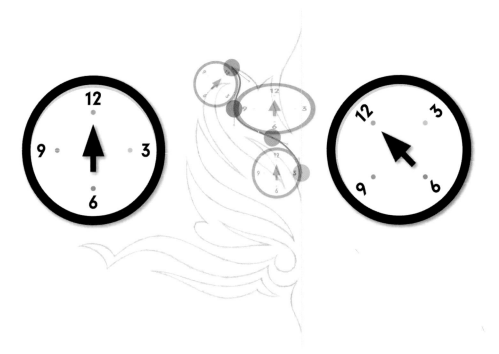

FIGURE 5.22 Using TCM, I begin to perform shape surveillance on my refined sketch, discerning my anchor point placement and orienting my clock to associate with the curves in my design, rotating it as needed.

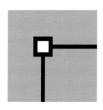

FIGURE 5.23 All the anchor points in this vector ornament design are the correct type, either corner or smooth, depending on their PPP. Corner anchor points are highlighted in orange. These were easy to discern.

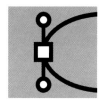

FIGURE 5.24 The smooth anchor points that control the curves, which bend smoothly from one side of the anchor point to the other, are highlighted in purple.

FIGURE 5.25 The final vector artwork for this visual identity utilized symmetry to form the final graphic mark.

The Yin and Yang of Anchor Points

Don't assume you'll get your TCM correct all the time. You simply won't. And when collaborating with others, you'll eventually be able to spot problem areas in their work as well. These are the most common problems:

- **Wrong anchor point:** Make sure you're using the correct type of anchor point in your path, either corner or smooth.

- **PPP isn't correct:** Some of your anchor points are still not in the ideal position to let you control the Bézier curves accurately. Go through your path and review each anchor point with TCM in mind, and double-check the PPP for each.

- **Not enough anchor points in path:** You haven't placed enough anchor points to form the shape accurately. You're probably struggling to form the exact Bézier curves for the path you need. Review your shape with TCM in mind and add anchor points on your path using the Add Anchor Point Tool (+) **(FIGURE 5.26)**.

- **Too many anchor points in path:** You've placed too many anchor points to form the shape with precision. It will be hard to control the path's flow and retain an elegant form. Review your shape with TCM in mind and remove the unnecessary anchor points from your path using the Delete Anchor Point Tool (–) **(FIGURE 5.27)**. A well-built vector shape should contain only the number of anchor points needed to pull it off. No more, no less.

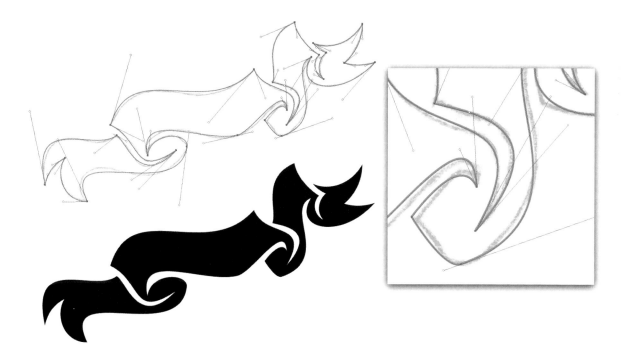

FIGURE 5.26 Not enough anchor points have been placed to build the banner shape accurately. A telltale sign is overextended Bézier handles.

FIGURE 5.27 Too many anchor points have been placed here, which ruins the graceful curves of the banner design. Managing all the anchor points and their small Bézier curve handles makes shaping the curves a major pain in the keister.

For example, the anchor points in the design shown in Figure 5.26 are actually in their correct PPP, but the path doesn't contain enough placed anchor points to build the shape precisely. A telltale sign you're not using enough anchor points is overextended Bézier curve handles.

Trying to build precise vector paths with overextended Bézier handles is like trying to paint a picture using a 6-foot-long brush. You couldn't stand close enough to your canvas to control your forms, and clearly the art would pay the price. The same is true with overextended Bézier handles. If you can't control your forms with precision, your design will wind up paying the price.

Many of the anchor points in the design shown in Figure 5.27 are in their correct PPP, but the path contains far too many anchor points to control the shape gracefully. It ends up looking clunky.

FIGURE 5.28 All anchor points are in their correct PPP, and the shape has the correct balance of anchor points needed to accurately create the final banner design. The end result is a more elegant form.

An unnecessary anchor point by definition can never be in a correct PPP. Delete the points from your path and simplify the shape.

Your ultimate goal is balance (**FIGURE 5.28**). After placing the anchor points and shaping the Bézier curves with their handles to form your art, you'll know immediately if you haven't placed enough or if you've placed too many to build it accurately. Be diligent in your surveillance, and you'll see massive improvements in your design.

The more you utilize TCM, the better you can avoid these common vector pitfalls. It's important to be able to recognize problems in your own design and the design of others you work with so you can improve the quality and consistently create at a higher level.

Deconstructing a Vector Monster

 Feeling overwhelmed? Let's deconstruct a real-world project with TCM and PPP in mind. Then you'll be ready to learn the various build methods presented in Chapter 6.

I created this illustrative design for a video production company. TCM and PPP played a key role in building core shapes for the final vector artwork.

Of course, smart vector build methods were also crucial in this project's success. We'll look at them more fully in the next chapter. That said, it's kind of like love and marriage: you can't have one without the other. That's why it's important to see everything in context, as follows:

1. **The Clockwork Method:** First, I performed shape surveillance and analyzed the shapes in my refined sketch using TCM (**FIGURE 5.29**).

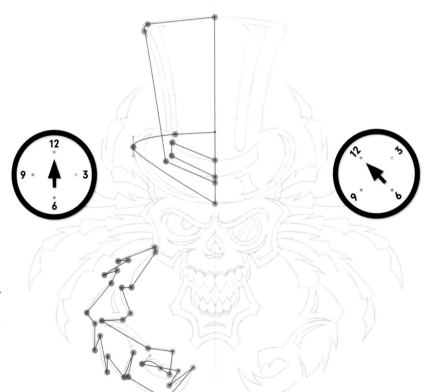

FIGURE 5.29 Using TCM, I placed my anchor points to form the core shapes needed to create the artwork. I didn't worry about adjusting handles at this point either.

2. **Prime Point Placement:** At this point, I zoomed in on my anchor points, moved them into more ideal locations to facilitate accurate Bézier curves, and adjusted the handles (**FIGURE 5.30**).

3. **Vector build methods:** I continued to build every vector shape needed to create my final art using TCM, PPP, and additional vector build methods that you'll learn about in Chapter 6 (**FIGURES 5.31** and **5.32**).

4. **Final artwork:** Once all my core shapes were built, I fused them together and moved on to coloring my vector art. Once coloring was done, I continued to use TCM, PPP, and additional vector build methods to build the various shapes needed for detailing the final artwork (**FIGURE 5.33**).

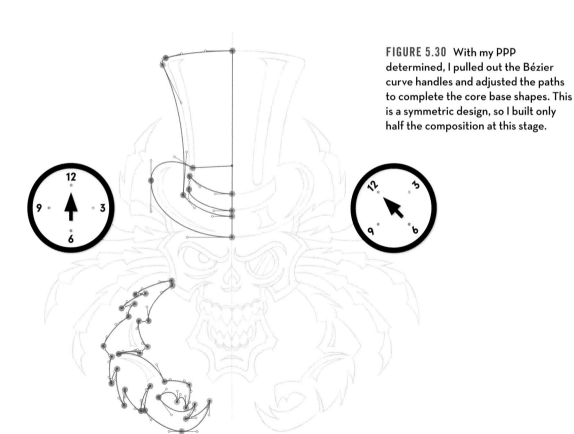

FIGURE 5.30 With my PPP determined, I pulled out the Bézier curve handles and adjusted the paths to complete the core base shapes. This is a symmetric design, so I built only half the composition at this stage.

FIGURE 5.31 I used the Point-by-Point Method for most of the vector shapes in this design. But I used the Ellipse tool in Adobe Illustrator to create others, such as the pupil.

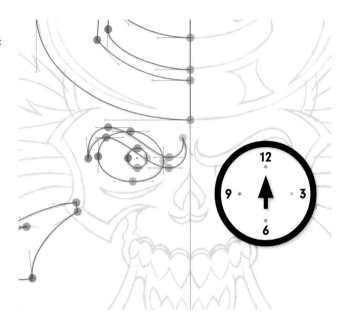

FIGURE 5.32 All the base vector shapes needed to create the final art built using TCM, PPP, and additional build methods covered in Chapter 6.

FIGURE 5.33 The final, monstrously unique visual identity for "Lord Maude Visionary Filmworx."

Practice Shape Discernment

When I spend a long time creating various projects, I've caught myself looking at shapes outside the context of work and thinking about how I'd build them as vector art. And it's these interludes that have inspired a creative exercise I want you to try.

Take notice of the various shapes you see around you: the shadow on someone's shirt, the profile of a face, the negative shapes found within a tree's branches. Once you've noticed a shape, ask yourself the following questions:

- Where would you place the points using TCM?

- What types of points would you need to use?

- What areas of the shape would need Bézier curves?

- How many shapes would it take to make up the final form?

Creative habits like this may be unorthodox, but I guarantee they'll improve your shape discernment.

Progressive Improvements

Building your vector shapes using the systematic creative process I've described can seem like a laborious task even for a simple design. Managing a complex design that can easily contain thousands of points and hundreds of paths might seem impossible. But with practice and time, it gets easier, and the process becomes second nature.

You'll never get your PPP absolutely correct the first time all the time. But the more you get into the habit of using TCM, the more consistently your anchor points will fall within the correct vector zip code as you build.

TCM and PPP are actually the first steps in the Point-by-Point Method that you'll learn about in Chapter 6. This process will help you even more. And in Chapter 8, "Art Directing Yourself," you'll learn this invaluable creative and managerial tool.

DESIGN DRILLS:
Spotting Clocks

When you get in the habit of using The Clock-work Method (TCM) to build your vector art, you'll start to see clocks in every vector-based design you look at, whether you designed it or not. And that's a good thing.

To kick-start the habit, let's take a look at a handful of designs from my own archive and see where the clocks show up.

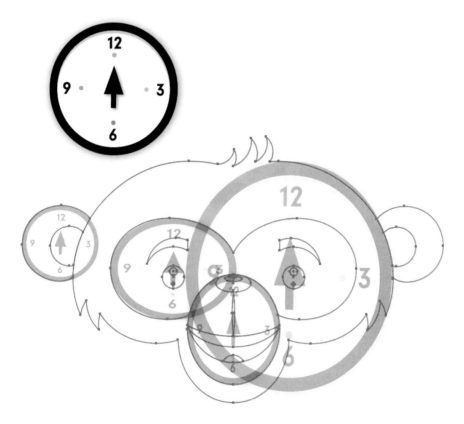

FIGURE 5.34 Sometimes the clock will form the entire shape, and sometimes it will just help create part of the shape.

FIGURE 5.35 This chimptastic monkey illustration was for a kid's play area.

FIGURE 5.36 Here I used TCM to guide me as I built letterforms in a hand-lettering design.

FIGURE 5.37 This logotype design exploration was for a line of Pepsi energy drinks.

FIGURE 5.38 Remember, this is a mental trick to help you discern your anchor point placements. Polly want a clock?

FIGURE 5.39 This was a package illustration exploration for ZuPreem, an exotic pet food line. The agency and the client loved it, but it ultimately failed in test marketing.

CHAPTER 6

Vector
Build Methods

As you build your design, it's important to clearly define your rules of creative engagement. This means choosing a build method that will not only allow you to work efficiently but also ensure that the final art is precise.

Chapter 5, "Shape Surveillance," covered two shape surveillance techniques: The Clockwork Method (TCM) and Prime Point Placement (PPP). This chapter will show you how to leverage both techniques using what I call the Point-by-Point Method. While TCM gets your points in the right neighborhood and PPP gets them to the right address, the Point-by-Point Method builds the actual structure.

In this chapter, you'll also learn the Shape-Building Method. This construction technique does just what it advertises: it builds shapes (with points conveniently already in place) using familiar Adobe Illustrator tools.

For the majority of your vector artwork, you'll need to use both the Point-by-Point Method and the Shape-Building Method. They work together like an artistic tag team. But how do you know when to use a given method? It depends on the shape you need to create.

• Use the Point-by-Point Method to create shapes that are free-flowing and organic. Forms with complex Bézier curves require this method (**FIGURE 6.1**).

• Use the Shape-Building Method to create shapes that are more geometric or iconic. Simple forms with 90-degree angles or circular or square shapes are ideal for the Shape-Building Method (**FIGURE 6.2**).

By the way, when your design requires a circular shape or another basic geometric form, don't worry about getting it perfect in your refined sketch. You can use the Shape-Building Method to do that job quickly later.

FIGURE 6.1 I designed this artwork, titled "Street Goblins," for a skateboard deck. I built the flames using the Point-by-Point Method and built the characters' eyes using ellipse shapes via the Shape-Building Method.

FIGURE 6.2 For this icon set, I relied heavily on the Shape-Building Method. Only a few elements required the Point-by-Point Method.

Before you begin to build in vector form, do your best to determine which parts will require the Point-by-Point Method and which will require the Shape-Building Method. The more you use both methods to create your vector art, the easier it will be to determine the one that's the best fit for a given shape.

In almost all my artwork, I use both methods in combination. Think of your craftsmanship like wine: your ability to discern which method to use—and your skill in using them—will improve with age.

Point-by-Point Method

Chapter 4, "Getting to the Points," focused on the good, the bad, and the ugly attributes of anchor points, and Chapter 5 showed you how to figure out where to place them.

The Point-by-Point Method takes the rough forms you created with TCM and PPP and transforms them into polished final art. Here's how it works.

One Point at a Time

When it comes to vector building, there's nothing more fundamental than building shapes one anchor point at a time—that's why it's called "Point-by-Point." It defines the modus operandi that most people use when working with vectors. I've created a four-step method that will help you optimize the process.

1. Do the rough build: Using TCM and PPP, place your anchor points in the correct locations to roughly form the shape you want to build (**FIGURE 6.3**). If an anchor point needs to be smooth, pull the Bézier handles out just enough so you can easily grab them later (in step 4). Don't try to refine the shape too much now; focus on placing the anchor points correctly.

2. Shape the path: Once your anchor points and their corresponding paths are in place, you have two choices regarding tools to shape the paths. You can use Illustrator's Anchor Point tool or the PathScribe tool (covered in Chapter 2, "Your Creative Armament"). Both have similar functions and let you grab anywhere on the path (between any two anchor points) and then push or pull it to form the desired shape (**FIGURE 6.4**), adjusting the Bézier curves as needed to match the vector path with the underlying drawing (**FIGURE 6.5**). Don't worry if you break your smooth anchor points; you can fix them in the next step if necessary and dial it in even more. The book images here show the Anchor Point tool only, but the videos included with this publication demonstrate both tools and explain why I prefer using the plug-in by Astute Graphics.

FIGURE 6.3 Place your anchor points using TCM and PPP as discussed in chapter 5.

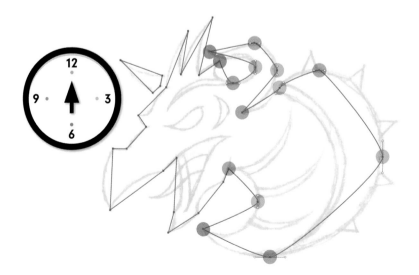

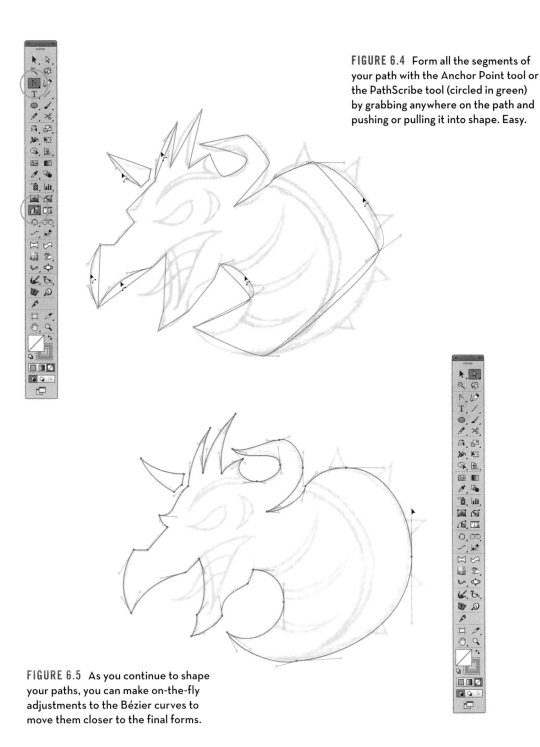

FIGURE 6.4 Form all the segments of your path with the Anchor Point tool or the PathScribe tool (circled in green) by grabbing anywhere on the path and pushing or pulling it into shape. Easy.

FIGURE 6.5 As you continue to shape your paths, you can make on-the-fly adjustments to the Bézier curves to move them closer to the final forms.

3. Smooth anchor points: Now, using the Direct Selection tool, select all anchor points that should be smooth—*not* corner points (**FIGURE 6.6**). Once you have them all selected, from the Control panel, use the rightmost button of the Convert option and click "Convert selected anchor points to smooth" (**FIGURE 6.7**). At this point, your vector art is ready to refine. (For more information about anchor points, see Chapter 4.)

4. Refine the shapes: Now focus more closely on the Bézier curves and pull their handles out to refine the path shape. Notice in **FIGURE 6.8** how the Bézier handles are parallel where necessary to ensure precise curves. Re-scrutinize your anchor point locations and make

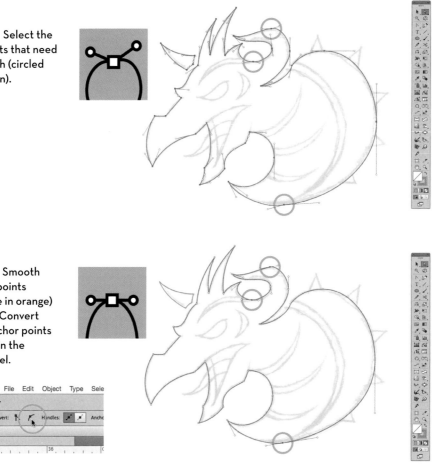

FIGURE 6.6 Select the anchor points that need to be smooth (circled here in green).

FIGURE 6.7 Smooth the anchor points (circled here in orange) by clicking "Convert selected anchor points to smooth" in the Control panel.

any necessary PPP corrections to form an accurate vector shape. (Review Prime Point Placement in Chapter 5.) Build the remaining shapes (**FIGURE 6.9**). **FIGURE 6.10** shows the final result.

These four steps might seem labor-intensive at first, but over time all the methods you learn in this book will become second nature to you. Once you get used to them, you won't have to think about each step of the process—they'll all be part of your natural workflow. Use these methods consistently, and you'll soon see your vector build times decrease and your precision and craftsmanship increase.

So, no whining: stay consistent and expect to struggle through this until it becomes your new normal. You won't be sorry.

FIGURE 6.8 Take your time and pay attention to the PPP and Bézier curve handles to ensure that they're not overextended. Shape the paths elegantly to match your drawing precisely.

FIGURE 6.9 Continue to build the remaining vector shapes needed to produce your final art. (Note: I created some of the new shapes, such as the arches that cut into the front and define the back of the character's neck, using the Shape-Building Method discussed later in this chapter.)

FIGURE 6.10 This shows the final vector artwork and several other avatar designs I created for an RPG game. My vector building utilized TCM, PPP, and the Point-by-Point Method, plus the Shape-Building Method (described later in this chapter).

Span the Distance Wisely

When you create a Bézier curve, you need to analyze the length of that curved path and determine how many anchor points you'll need to form it precisely.

Getting the anchor points right means using enough to get the job done accurately, but not so many that it's hard to control the form of the vector path. Chapters 4 and 5 discussed this tangentially, but since it's a core aspect of the Point-by-Point Method, it's important to focus on it more specifically now. **FIGURES 6.11–6.13** show how to find the balance between not enough and too many anchor points. Keep TCM and PPP in mind.

FIGURE 6.11 I used four anchor points to form the Bézier curve elegantly and with precise control.

FIGURE 6.12 While it's technically correct to form the same type of Bézier curve using only two points, aesthetically it's wonky because it just doesn't produce an elegant curve. The handlebars are extended too far, causing the path to appear flat in some areas. This level of scrutinizing detail is what separates the pros from the amateurs. A pro will take the time to refine the shape, whereas an amateur will usually say, "This is good enough."

FIGURE 6.13 Final
vector artwork for this
ornamental design.

FIGURE 6.13 Final
vector artwork for this
ornamental design.

Shape-Building Method

Creating your artwork with one continuous path, Point-by-Point, isn't
always practical, nor is it an efficient use of your time. This is where the
Shape-Building Method comes in. It's a simple and fast way to build
precise shapes using one or more of the following tools in Illustrator:
the Rectangle tool (M), the Ellipse tool (L), and the Pathfinder panel
(Shift-Command-F9 or Shift-Control-F9). It's faster to build simple
geometric shapes using the shape tools because they form the entire
shape needed with all anchor points in place automatically. It's also more
precise than manually trying to position each anchor point on a path and
then adjusting multiple Bézier curves.

Here's how to use the Shape-Building Method to create a palm leaf in
three simple steps:

1. Basic vector shapes: Your sketches needn't be refined if the
    shape you're creating is a simple one, like the palm leaf shown in
    FIGURE 6.14. Create the base art using the Point-by-Point Method
    and then switch to the Shape-Building Method: make the notches

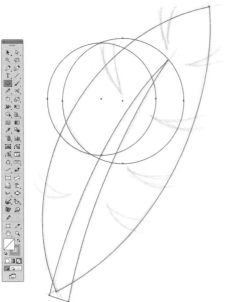

FIGURE 6.14 Use the Ellipse tool (L) to create two circles to form the notch in the palm leaf.

FIGURE 6.15 The Ellipse tool (L) and the Pathfinder panel (Shift-Command-F9 or Shift-Control-F9) can be simple but powerful vector-building tools. You can use them to create all the shapes needed to form the leaf's notch details.

in the palm leaf with the Ellipse tool (L) and create two circle shapes that match the contour of the sketch. (See Chapter 2 for more information about this tool.)

2. Pathfinder panel (Shift-Command-F9 or Shift-Control-F9): Select the two circles that make up the notch in the palm leaf and click the Minus Front button in the Pathfinder panel (circled in green in **FIGURE 6.15**). This will create a new shape that is formed by the top circle punching through the bottom circle (think of a cookie cutter). Copy this notch shape and size and rotate it to form the remaining notches in the leaf, as shown in **FIGURE 6.16**. (See Chapter 2 for more information on Pathfinder functions.)

FIGURE 6.16 Copy the notch shape and rotate it to create the other notches in the palm leaf.

3. Final shape building: Once you have all the necessary stem and notch shapes in place, select them all (Shift-V) and then click the Unite button (circled in green) in the Pathfinder panel (Shift-Command-F9 or Shift-Control-F9) (**FIGURES 6.17–6.19**).

The palm leaf is part of the repeat pattern design shown in **FIGURE 6.20**. This artwork is a good example of using both the Point-by-Point Method and the Shape-Building Method.

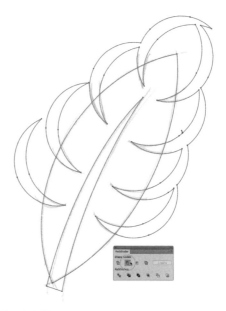

FIGURE 6.17 Select all the notch shapes and the stem shape and then click the Unite button (circled in green) in the Pathfinder panel. (Watch the "Shape-Building Method" video.)

FIGURE 6.18 Select the new vector shape and the base palm leaf shape (Shift-V) and then click the Minus Front button (highlighted in green) in the Pathfinder panel (Shift-Command-F9 or Shift-Control-F9) to form the final art (as shown in Figure 6.17).

FIGURE 6.19 The final vector shape of the palm leaf, created using the Point-by-Point Method and the Shape-Building Method.

FIGURE 6.20 "Tiki Lounge" repeat pattern design.

When to Use Which Method

The type of shape you're trying to create will dictate whether it's best to use the Shape-Building Method or the Point-by-Point Method. Rarely, if ever, will you build your entire project using one or the other. For most of your projects, you'll start building your vector art with the Point-by-Point Method, and sometime during the build process, you'll get to a specific part of your design that will lend itself to the Shape-Building Method.

It's all about discerning the shape you need to build and realizing when it's easier and more precise to create a certain shape using the shape tools and when it's better to manually place anchor points and adjust Bézier curves. Let's take a look at another design that required both methods (**FIGURES 6.21–6.26**).

FIGURE 6.21 I used this refined sketch of a character design as a guide for building my vector shapes.

FIGURE 6.22 Because I took the time to draw out the shapes, I knew how to build them, which eliminated guesswork. I used Point-by-Point Method building to create the eyebrow and the Ellipse tool (L) to create the circular shapes that make up the eye. I used the Point-by-Point Method to build the eyebrow because it's more free-form and can't be built using shape tools. I used the Ellipse tool (L) to create the eyes because they consist of simple, geometric shapes that would be harder to build manually, one anchor point at a time. These are the types of simple build decisions you'll make on the fly as you create your vector forms in Illustrator.

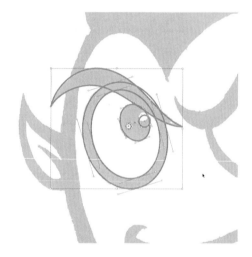

FIGURE 6.23 I continued to use the Ellipse tool (L) to create the character's arm and hand. The shapes that make up the arm and hand are more geometric than organic, so they naturally lend themselves to using the shape tools instead of manually positioning the anchor points one at a time. Using the same method as in the palm leaf example earlier in this chapter (Figures 6.14–6.17), I selected two circular shapes at a time and clicked the Minus Front button (circled in green) in the Pathfinder panel (Shift-Command-F9 or Shift-Control-F9) to create the final arm and hand shown in Figure 6.24.

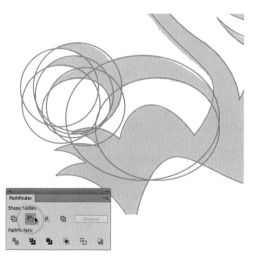

FIGURE 6.24 The final Shape-Building results.

FIGURE 6.25 I continued using TCM and PPP (covered in Chapter 5) to discern the best anchor point placement during the Point-by-Point build process. I leveraged the Shape-Building Method to create the character's other arm, teeth, wing, and tongue, along with the corners of his mouth and one of his horns. I created everything else with the Point-by-Point Method.

FIGURE 6.26 The final character design was part of an ad agency pitch for a Fanta Phantom character Halloween promotion.

Using both vector build methods will help you master the creation of any shape. Don't let a complex shape intimidate you. Instead, approach it with creative confidence, knowing you can tag-team any vector challenge.

Throwaway Shapes

When you use the Shape-Building Method, you'll create certain shapes for no other reason than to move another shape further along in the build process. These sacrificial shapes are important, but they never appear in the final art (**FIGURES 6.27–6.31**).

FIGURE 6.27 I used the Ellipse tool (L) to create this eye for a tribal owl design. With two of the circular shapes selected, I clicked the Minus Front button (circled in green) in the Pathfinder panel (Shift-Command-F9 or Shift-Control-F9) to finish off the last shape needed for the eye.

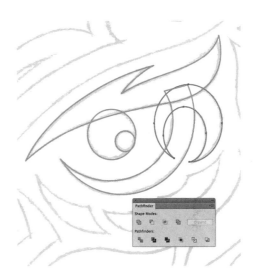

FIGURE 6.28 The end result of my shape building was this moon shape. I wanted to retain most of the shape's form but needed to trim off some of it—that's where I used a throwaway shape.

FIGURE 6.29 I created a rectangle, selected both shapes and then clicked the Minus Front button (circled in green) in the Pathfinder panel (Shift-Command-F9 or Shift-Control-F9).

FIGURE 6.30 With the throwaway shape removed, the final vector shape needed for the tribal owl illustration appeared. On a design like this, I can easily perform this same technique about a hundred times before I'm done with it.

 FIGURE 6.31 The final tribal owl illustration. To learn more about illustrating in this style, check out my tribal illustration course at www.drawingvectorgraphics.com.

VectorScribe Plug-in

In Chapter 2, you learned that the VectorScribe plug-in can be a valuable tool for creating vector artwork. It also has some powerful features for editing and refining your artwork.

When you create art using the Shape-Building Method, your final shape might need some additional refining. The VectorScribe plug-in by Astute Graphics can help you easily get that job done.

Remove Redundant Points

As I griped in Chapter 2, Illustrator contains a bug in the Pathfinder panel that creates redundant points in your artwork. This means that one point literally sits on top of another. When you select a shape, it might look normal, but these redundancies can cause problems later.

The VectorScribe plug-in contains a function called Remove Redundant Points that can remove all such duplicate anchor points in your entire illustration or design. Let's take a closer look at how this plug-in works (**FIGURE 6.32**).

FIGURE 6.32 Select your vector shape or your entire design as shown. On the VectorScribe panel, you'll see the number of points in your artwork on the left (circled in orange). If an exclamation mark appears on the right (circled in orange), your art contains redundant points. With your art still selected, simply click the exclamation mark. You'll immediately see a new total point count appear on the panel, revealing how many redundant points were removed from your artwork. In this specific case, we removed four redundant points.

In the VectorScribe plug-in preferences, you can choose to have redundant points automatically removed (circled in orange). I prefer having this function turned off since at times I purposely snap to points in order to build certain content.

Smart Remove

Sometimes when you build vector art, whether by the Point-by-Point or Shape-Building Method, you inevitably add extra points to your vector paths. Or maybe you decide later that you simply don't need one or more of the anchor points you initially placed.

You can use VectorScribe's Smart Remove tool to remove extra anchor points from a path and still retain the art's shape. This is a simple but useful feature that Illustrator lacks. Let's look at how it works (**FIGURES 6.33–6.35**).

FIGURE 6.33 When I added a gray outline to this school mascot design, extra anchor points were added when I expanded the stroke. To remove them, I simply selected all the anchor points I wanted to remove (circled in orange) and clicked the Smart Remove button on the VectorScribe panel (circled in orange).

FIGURE 6.34 Notice how the vector shape retains its original form after the extra anchor points are removed. This is why this feature is called Smart Remove. I often use this feature when I build and sometimes use it with Prime Point Placement (PPP) to optimize and refine my anchor point locations as well.

FIGURE 6.35 Trying the same kind of anchor point removal using Illustrator's Remove Selected Anchor Point function in the Control panel (circled here in orange) ruins the original shape of the design. It's not smart at all. In fact, I'd give it an F-minus and put it in vector detention indefinitely.

E Pluribus Buildum

You've probably seen the phrase *E Pluribus Unum*, which is Latin for "Out of many, one," on U.S. currency.

This saying can also apply to the process of building vector designs. As you create your vector shapes using the Point-by-Point and Shape-Building Methods, you can also benefit from dissecting your design into more manageable individual shapes and combining them later into the final shape you need.

Chapter 3, "Analog Methods in a Digital Age," touched on this, and you'll notice it in many of the images in this book as well.

Dissecting Your Design

A variety of complex shapes can make up any design. In a custom logotype, for example, the shapes also have to be consistent and precise in order to make the letterforms readable.

A project like this is made far easier by dissecting it into smaller, individual shapes. This lets you focus on each part and render it accurately.

When I analyze a design concept like the one in **FIGURES 6.36** and **6.37**, I dissect the forms into more manageable pieces (**FIGURES 6.38** and **6.39**). This helps to maintain the continuity of the content. For example, I used the horizontal width of the shapes in the letter "H" in the word "Church" to guide my building on other letterform widths, such as the "B," "U," and "R." If I'd tried to build each letterform as a single path, it would have taken a lot more time and effort on my part to pull it off with precision (**FIGURES 6.40–6.41**).

Whether you're building your design using the Point-by-Point Method or the Shape-Building Method or both, dissecting your design is a way to make the whole creative process easier.

FIGURE 6.36 A rough sketch of a logotype design direction.

FIGURE 6.37 I used this refined drawing as a guide to build the vector shapes in Illustrator.

FIGURE 6.38 Focusing on individual shapes and dissecting them into even smaller individual shapes helped me build the vector art faster and with more precision.

FIGURE 6.39 This image shows all the individual shapes that make up this logotype design. To form the final shape, I combined the individual shapes and punched out others using the Pathfinder panel (Shift-Command-F9 or Shift-Control-F9).

FIGURE 6.40 As I worked, I noticed some areas of the design that could be improved. This image shows the shapes I added to or subtracted from the letterforms to refine the design. This topic is covered in greater depth in Chapter 8, "Art Directing Yourself."

FIGURE 6.41 The final logotype design. Note that I removed the inner curls on the "C" letterforms to improve readability.

Symmetry Is Your Friend

There's one additional build technique you can use, in combination with the Point-by-Point and Shape-Building Methods, to really speed up your work: working symmetrically.

When you create symmetrical artwork, you only have to build half of the art (top left in **FIGURE 6.42**). From that you'll be able to create the entire finished piece by simply cloning the shapes you need and flipping them using the Reflect tool.

Here's how:

1. Create vector art based on your refined sketch. Select the vector shapes (V-Shift) (top left of Figure 6.42).

2. With the vector shapes selected, position the Reflect tool (O) on one of the center anchor points (circled in red). Hold down the Shift key and drag the cursor to the left to flip the art. (The flipped vector art is colored green in the top right of Figure 6.42.)

3. Now that you have all your shapes in place, select them and click the Unite button (to merge shapes) or the Minus Front button (to eliminate shapes) to create all of the final vector forms needed for your design (bottom left of Figure 6.42).

The symmetrical character art used the Point-by-Point Method, the Shape-Building Method, and symmetry to create the final design shown at the bottom right of Figure 6.42. The more you're able to combine the various build methods covered in this book, the more productive your workflow will be (**FIGURES 6.43–6.52**).

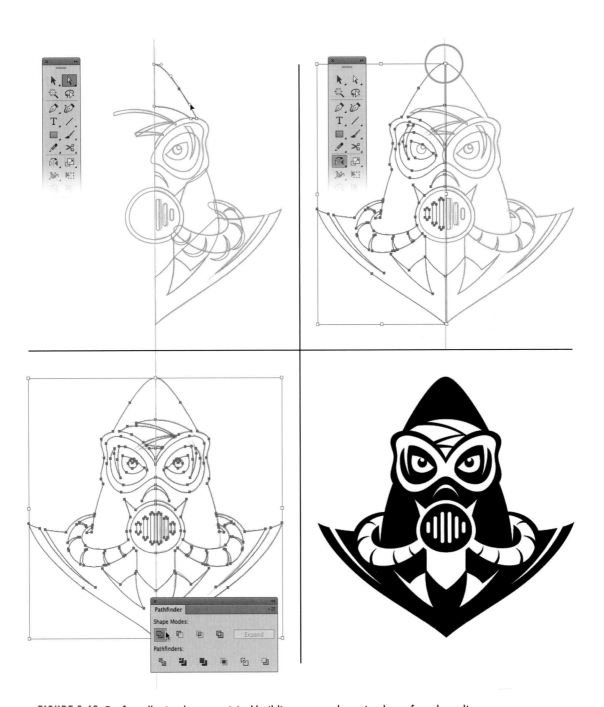

FIGURE 6.42 Profoundly simple symmetrical building can produce simply profound results.

FIGURE 6.43 The thumbnail sketch for an evil clown illustration.

FIGURE 6.44 I used this refined sketch as a guide to build my vector shapes in Illustrator. Nonsymmetrical elements like the hair on the forehead are always good to add to an illustration like this.

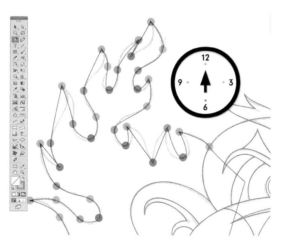

FIGURE 6.45 I discerned my anchor point locations using TCM and PPP (covered in Chapter 5) and then used the Point-by-Point Method to form the flaming hair shape.

FIGURE 6.46 The rendered vector art precisely matches my underlying drawing. I continued to use this method as I built the rest of the vector shapes.

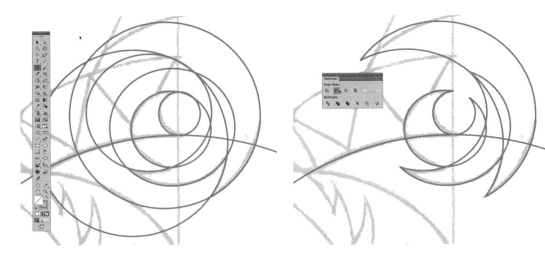

FIGURE 6.47 Using the Shape-Building Method, I created six circular shapes with the Ellipse tool (L) to form part of the hair in my illustration.

FIGURE 6.48 I then selected the various shapes and clicked the Minus Front button in the Pathfinder panel (Shift-Command-F9 or Shift-Control-F9) to knock out the sections of the curve that I didn't want showing up in my final graphic. The result is a curved shape that looks more like hair than a circle.

FIGURE 6.49 As I continued to build, I selected the shapes and clicked the Unite function in the Pathfinder panel (Shift-Command-F9 or Shift-Control-F9) along with another throwaway shape to form the tuft of hair.

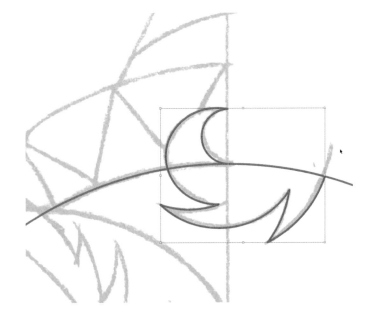

FIGURE 6.50 This image shows all of the final, symmetrically planned shapes.

FIGURE 6.51 I cloned (Command-C or Control-C, Command-F or Control-F) the vector shapes and flipped them using the Reflect tool (O). Once the shapes were reflected, I selected various shapes and clicked the Unite button in the Pathfinder panel (Shift-Command-F9 or Shift-Control-F9) to form all the vector shapes needed for the final artwork. I removed redundant or extra anchor points using the VectorScribe plug-in. (Review the VectorScribe plug-in instructions covered earlier in this chapter.)

FIGURE 6.52 I titled the final artwork "Tickles, the Evil Clown." Tickles won several illustration awards, and a large-format print was part of a gallery show at the New York Society of Illustrators.

A Healthy Creative Process

I isolated my various build methods in this chapter so that I could walk you through each one individually. I then explained how to use the methods together in the greater context of a systematic creative process.

But the creative process isn't always orderly. Many times a project will require you to revisit earlier steps to arrive at the final vector art. A good example of this was documented in Figures 3.34–3.36. The same will be true in your own projects as you begin to use the Point-by-Point Method and the Shape-Building Method covered in this chapter.

A healthy creative process should be flexible, adaptable, honest, and open to the use of any method at any given time to improve the final result.

FIELD NOTES

Skullduggery

In the exercise files you'll find a file called Skullduggery.ai, and within this file you'll find eight basic vector shapes.

- Three circles

- Three rectangles

- One square

- One triangle

Your creative challenge is to take the eight shapes included in this file and create a skull graphic using the Shape-Building Method covered in this chapter. You can proportionately scale the shapes, but you cannot distort or skew them.

How did you do? Compare your vector building with the solution file included in the folder for this challenge.

DESIGN DRILLS:
Fast and Easy

As discussed earlier in this chapter, dissecting your vector building into smaller, more manageable shapes makes the whole process of forming your art easier and leads to faster build times, especially when you're creating complex designs.

In this section, I've gathered together a few of my more complex designs so you can see how I diced up each one (**FIGURES 6.53–6.58**).

FIGURE 6.53 I created this ornament design by dissecting the overall form into multiple shapes. I united the various parts in one larger united path using the tools in the Pathfinder panel.

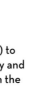

FIGURE 6.54 I used the Reflect tool (O) to reflect the ornament design horizontally and then reflected it again vertically to form the complete frame motif.

FIGURE 6.55 Symmetry is another way to cut your build time since it essentially eliminates half your workload. This example shows half of a design for a tribal bear that I created and then completed using symmetry.

FIGURE 6.56 The complete tribal bear illustration for a book cover exploration.

FIGURE 6.57 Distilling this complex tiger illustration into smaller shapes made it far easier to flesh out. I was able to work faster while staying focused on the smaller details.

FIGURE 6.58 The final white tiger illustration, which was commissioned by a nonprofit for a poster to promote a diabetes research fundraiser.

CHAPTER 7

Style Appropriate

There's a common misconception in the creative community that you need a signature visual style to gain fame, fortune, and future work. There's no such thing as one-style-fits-all design. In fact, forcing yourself to approach every design project with the same style will limit your opportunities *and* your growth as a creative professional.

As a designer, it's important to study the intended audience for any project you take on and to choose a style that speaks authentically to that audience (**FIGURE 7.1**). Your design might be aesthetically pleasing, win numerous awards, and even be based on a clever concept, but if it doesn't resonate with the people its intended for, it's merely eye candy—delicious, perhaps, but not very good for you or your client's business.

Be creatively proactive and leverage diverse styles in order to produce work that not only meets your clients' needs but exceeds them. It's an effective way to stay relevant in an industry that becomes more competitive every year.

"Failure is not fatal, but failure to change might be."
—JOHN WOODEN

Design Chameleons

I love expanding my creative horizons by exploring new styles. Being able to work in a variety of styles has brought me a broader range of projects and clientele. Over the years, I've become a design chameleon of sorts. Many art directors have hired me because I'm able to offer several directions to help them explore potential solutions.

With each new project, I decide early on which specific style or styles I'll use so I can prepare any reference material I might need. If the style is a more complex one, I determine how long it will take to create and what vector build methods will work best to produce the final art. Having this information before I put pencil or pen to paper is invaluable.

Let's walk through four real-world projects, each of which required me to leverage a different but appropriate style to produce the design the client needed.

FIGURE 7.1 Shown clockwise from top left are a licensing image for Wayne Enterprises, an illustration for a T-shirt design, a design for a skate graphic, a brand character design and lettering for a microbrewery, a tribal illustration just for fun, and hand-lettering for an editorial article. The style of each is appropriate for its intended audience (opposite page).

FIGURE 7.2 Referencing a rough thumbnail, I drew out a refined sketch of the linear line icon.

Linear Line Style

The linear line style was first made popular by Pablo Picasso in his sketches and more recently has become a favorite concept within the design industry for marketing products as diverse as insurance, coffee, medical services, real estate, cars, and, as demonstrated in this project, banking (**FIGURES 7.2–7.14**). This style was appropriate for this client because it worked for print collateral and could easily be animated for TV spots.

FIGURE 7.3 I made refined sketches of all the linear line icons I'd be creating. Doing this helped me pin down exactly what I'd have to build in vector form and eliminated guesswork.

FIGURE 7.4 I created most of the linear icons using the Point-by-Point Method, but on this light bulb, I was able to use the Shape-Building Method as well.

FIGURE 7.5 I finessed my Bézier curve to polish off the vector path.

FIGURE 7.6 Next, I chose a weight for the final stroke size that would look good whether the icon was used big or small.

FIGURE 7.7 I re-created the bank's logo in the same style of the icons since it would appear in the same context as the icons and type.

FIGURE 7.8 I drew this icon using the Point-by-Point Method.

FIGURE 7.9 These images show the revisions I made to satisfy the client's request that the nose be rounded off.

FIGURE 7.10 The client also requested that the mouth span the whole face, so I edited my vector art as shown here.

FIGURE 7.11 The client didn't like one of the eyes and asked that the loop in the nose be removed. Overall, the changes were reasonable, and I think they improved the final icon, which is the whole point of art direction.

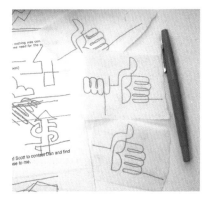

FIGURE 7.12 The client decided another icon of a hand was needed, so I quickly sketched out this concept.

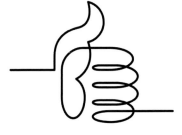

FIGURE 7.13 The final linear line hand, giving a thumbs-up.

FIGURE 7.14 This style lends itself to animation in which the line draws itself. The ad agency used my linear art in TV spots for the bank, as well as in print collateral and signage. For more information about this style, check out my "Drawing Vector Graphics: Linear Line Illustration" course at www.DrawingVectorGraphics.com.

Segmented Style

 If I had a signature style, it would be this one, which was influenced by the work of Jim Flora, an art director at RCA Victor in the 1950s. I've used this segmented style on projects for Adobe, a national restaurant chain, a book publisher, several magazines, and, in this example, a self-promotional product called Keyboard Characters (**FIGURES 7.15–7.26**).

FIGURE 7.15 My thumbnail sketches for a Keyboard Character called Riled Rover.

FIGURE 7.16 My refined sketch for Riled Rover. Sometimes I redraw a sketch and tape it on top of a previous iteration, as shown here.

FIGURE 7.17 My refined sketch, ready to be scanned in and used.

FIGURE 7.18 I built most of the vector paths using the Point-by-Point Method but kept The Clockwork Method in mind as I placed the anchor points. On the teeth, I used the Shape-Building Method via the Ellipse tool (L) and the Pathfinder panel (Command-Shift-F9 or Control-Shift-F9).

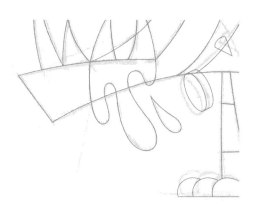

FIGURE 7.19 Notice how I built the vector art to match my drawing. I deviated from the drawing only in areas that were easier to build digitally, such as the spikes, dog tag, and toes, all of which I created using the shape-building tools in Illustrator.

FIGURE 7.20 The completed base vector shapes.

FIGURE 7.21 Next, I began to work out the flat fill colors.

FIGURE 7.22 The final art for the Riled Rover Keyboard Character.

FIGURE 7.23 These are three more Keyboard Characters: Pet Monster, DZGN-BOT, and Feed Your Imagination.

FIGURE 7.24 Press proof for the Keyboard Character set.

FIGURE 7.25 Color proof for the Riled Rover Keyboard Character.

FIGURE 7.26 The finished Keyboard Characters self-promotional product. You can order your own set at www.GlitschkaStudios.com.

Tribal Tattoo Style

Years ago, I would meet with a group of other illustrators once a month and each of us would illustrate our own take on an agreed-upon topic. One month it was tattoos. I've always liked the graphic nature of tribal tattoos, so I decided to draw a face.

That simple creative experiment led to a style that I've used for book covers, custom tattoo designs, energy drinks, beer branding, stickers, and, as shown in **FIGURES 7.27–7.34**, a product design for a company called InkDot. The tribal tattoo style was appropriate for this client's product line, which uses a range of artistic styles to cater to a wide range of people.

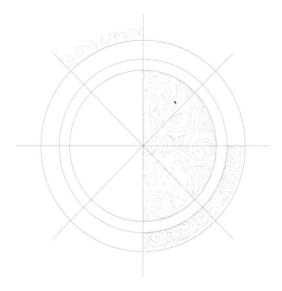

FIGURE 7.27 For this tribal design, I took my rough thumbnail sketch, scanned it in, and created a template layout to guide my refined drawing.

FIGURE 7.28 I placed vellum over the template layout and began drawing a refined sketch. This precise drawing guided my vector-building efforts and aligned with the template guides I set up previously. A mechanical pencil aided in this effort.

FIGURES 7.29 As I moved back to digital and started to build on top of the refined sketch, I used the Astute Graphics VectorScribe tool to form most of the vector shapes.

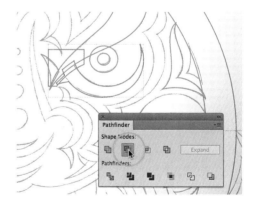

FIGURE 7.30 I used the Shape-Building Method to form the eye in this design. Pathfinder allows me to work fast and build precisely.

FIGURE 7.31 The final symmetric base vectors. You can see I built only half the design. I used the selection tool to select the shapes, clone them, and reflect them to form the whole design.

FIGURE 7.32 Once I'd cloned and reflected all the vector shapes, I was ready to explore color.

FIGURE 7.33 The final flat color application printed on a ceramic plate. I titled this design "Dark Matter."

FIGURE 7.34 I also took the vector design into Photoshop and texturized it. I used this iteration for throw pillows, art prints, and wallpaper. For more information about textures, check out my "Creating and Using Textures in Design" course at www.DrawingVectorGraphics.com.

Graphic Style

Not all projects require an extensive illustrative approach. A simple and iconic style may be more appropriate for projects such as custom lettering, icons, and ornaments. I used it in a logo design for an Italian animation company (**FIGURES 7.35–7.42**). Keeping the style simple meant that the logo could be more easily adapted to a broad range of applications without running into readability problems.

But the main reason I picked this stylistic direction was because it adhered to my design philosophy regarding logo identity: Simple is better.

FIGURE 7.35 To start, I roughed out a symmetrical thumbnail for the logo design, scanned it in, and mocked up the whole face so I could sketch out the type. (*Bocca* means "mouth" in Italian.) I used this rough version to draw my refined sketch.

FIGURE 7.36 The refined sketch. Since the design was symmetrical, I had to build only half of the character's face.

FIGURE 7.37 The spacing between the elements was too tight in three places (circled in orange), which created visual tension, so I made myself a mental note to balance out those areas as I moved forward. (See Chapter 8, "Art Directing Yourself," for more about visual tension.)

FIGURE 7.38 I created most of this design using the Point-by-Point Method, but I used the Shape-Building Method in a few spots, such as the nostril and the pupil of the eye.

FIGURES 7.39 Once I'd created all the symmetrical vectors, I selected all the shapes and flipped them using the Reflect tool (O) to form the final base vector artwork.

FIGURE 7.40 Next I worked out the color scheme for the logo. Notice how I purposely left out certain details like whiskers. Knowing what to leave out of a design is just as important as knowing what to include.

FIGURES 7.41 Small details can add a lot to a design. Just adding the small hot spots (white circles) to the eyes breathed life into this logo.

FIGURE 7.42 The final Big Bocca logo design.

FIELD NOTES

Create a Style Board

A simple creative habit that will help you recognize appropriate styles for various genres is to take notice of them in other contexts. Start collecting samples of different styles you come across and build a style board with them.

A bulletin board in your work area or office is a convenient place to hang up different styles you like and might want to try in your own work. With an established collection, you won't forget about particular styles, and the board will build your creative confidence as you move forward.

A smart designer will leverage various styles to be a more effective visual communicator. If you find yourself stuck in the same old visual rut, then move in a new direction. Try a completely different style on your next project instead of creatively capitulating to the same tired routine.

DESIGN DRILLS:
Use It or Lose It

A creative process in which you draw out an idea, refine it, and then build from it in vector form—making improvements along the way—will be successful only if you apply it consistently on every project.

In other words, if you don't use the methods covered in this book routinely, as in *every day*, then you won't see the benefits over time. Use it or lose it; it's up to you.

FIGURES 7.43 and **7.44** use all the methods I've outlined in this book, but my analog work in the drawing phase improved my vector results.

FIGURE 7.43 Investing the time up front to draw, redraw, and refine your design until you have it all worked out will save you many hours of frustration when you move to digital and start building it. So, don't cut corners; embrace the struggle.

FIGURE 7.44 This illustration was inspired by my love of 1980s power ballads, guitar riffs, and fashionable Doc Martens. Ah, the memories.

CHAPTER 8

Art Directing
Yourself

There's a plethora of creative professionals in the communications industry, and they're all competing with one another in a
global marketplace, with the Internet serving as an ever-present
facilitator. Design opinions shift quickly, trends take flight, and
designers can showcase their work to more people worldwide
than ever before.

What will set your work apart in this graphic cacophony is your ability to scrutinize your work honestly, admit its shortcomings, revise your creative process, and improve your capabilities with each new project. In other words, you have to know how to art direct yourself.

Art direction isn't so much about correcting mistakes as it is about shaping perceptions. When you art direct yourself, your goal is to craft an aesthetic that achieves the desired response from the intended audience.

Think of it this way: Design tends to be a wonderful paradox where objective methods produce creative work that is viewed subjectively.

Fresh Eyes Effect

As a creative person, you can spend so much time looking at your work that it can be difficult to detect potential problems. Everything starts to blend together. When this happens, honest critique is missed and, with it, needed improvements.

This is a dangerous situation because it can result in subpar work. It also opens the door for your clients to notice problems and directly associate that lack of attention to detail with your creative services.

A simple way to avoid this situation is to use what I call the *fresh eyes effect*. When you reach a particular stage in your work, set it aside and turn your attention to something completely different for a while. An hour is ideal, but even 15 minutes can be enough to purge your mind's cache and refresh your eyes. When you approach your work later, you can scrutinize it anew and more easily see areas that need improvement. The number and kinds of tweaks you'll need to make will vary depending on your ability and what stage of the creative process the work is in.

When I was hired by a beverage company to illustrate a tribal tattoo-styled Aztec warrior, I first drew out and refined my sketch, as shown in **FIGURE 8.1**. I spent a lot of time working on this, but something just didn't feel right. Whenever that happens, it's a sign for me to set down

FIGURE 8.1 My initial refined sketch for the tribal tattoo-styled Aztec warrior.

FIGURE 8.2 My new refined sketch, with improvements made after looking at it with fresh eyes.

the project, walk away, and approach it later with fresh eyes. So I shelved the job and decided to pick it up again the next day.

The next morning, I looked at the sketch with fresh eyes and was able to pinpoint the problems: The proportion of the overall head seemed too thin, the ethnicity didn't look right, and the eyes were getting lost in the detail, so they were less captivating than they could be. I made the needed corrections, and the overall result was an authentic vibe that was missing in the initial refined sketch (**FIGURE 8.2**).

With my refined sketch dialed in, I was able to get it approved by the client and move forward with building the design in vector form (**FIGURE 8.3**).

In a creative environment that demands an accelerated timeline, using fresh eyes may seem unrealistic. But it's not impossible. Even allowing yourself a small amount of time to reset your creative perspective is better than none at all (**FIGURE 8.4**).

FIGURE 8.3 Building the vector shapes, using The Clockwork Method, Prime Point Placement, and other techniques outlined in Chapters 5 and 6.

FIGURE 8.4 The final vector artwork used on the packaging of an energy drink. Fresh eyes helped me create work that served my client better.

Your Inner Art Director

Self-art direction isn't limited to the drawing stage. It should take place *throughout the entire creative process.*

As a responsible designer, you should always be looking for opportunities to improve and grow creatively. So, you'll want to continually make micro-adjustments and conceive better ways to pull things off as you create your vector artwork on any given project.

Listen to your inner art director and be sensitive to the sometimes-fleeting feelings that reveal themselves as you work. Don't ignore them—correct the problems that they uncover. They may seem insignificant, but, as a designer, you should care about this level of detail because no one else will ever be as passionate about your work as you are.

As I work through a project, I pay close attention when that inner voice declares, "Something doesn't feel right." Even if I don't understand why at that moment, I'll stop and give myself some time to figure out what to do next. This type of internal conversation happens with every project I work on (**FIGURES 8.5–8.9**).

FIGURE 8.5 This is a thumbnail sketch for a germ character for a licensing company. In general, it encapsulates the idea I'm after, but my inner art director is telling me to refine the form so that the shapes I'll use to build it in vector form are clear, eliminating guesswork.

FIGURE 8.6 This is my refined sketch. I've thoroughly defined the shapes needed to create the character in vector form and have identified exact proportions. I'm ready to start building digitally.

FIGURE 8.7 As I start building my vector shapes, my inner art director tells me to keep the tentacles separate from the body, rather than fusing them. I also add other shapes in the eye that will make detailing easier.

FIGURE 8.8 I choose a tonal family (See Chapter 9, "Basic Coloring and Detailing") and begin composing my color palette to create a nice contrast between the shapes that make up this character.

FIGURE 8.9 My inner art director played a huge role in deciding which details—such as shading, highlights, and gradients (more on these in Chapter 9)—to add to create the final illustration.

No one's work is perfect when it hits the page. As you collaborate with others during your career, they'll no doubt point out problems in your work that you're blind to. Don't take offense; it's important to absorb all forms of feedback so you can learn, grow, and become the best you can possibly be.

The fact that you're reading this book shows that you're ready to accept this sort of input, and that's a good sign. In time, being your own art director will become second nature.

Avoid Visual Tension

Shape, and thereby form, is important when creating vector artwork. But how a shape relates to another shape within any given design context is of equal or even greater importance. You might produce a well-crafted and precise shape, but if it's not well balanced with other shapes in a composition, it won't stand up aesthetically. I define this type of problematic shape relationship as visual tension.

Look at **FIGURE 8.10**. Where does your eye automatically go when you look at these shapes? Your eye will probably return to the area circled in red in **FIGURE 8.11** because that's where visual tension exists.

FIGURE 8.10 Look at this graphic and let your eye naturally go where it wants to go.

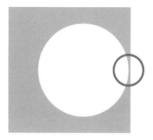

FIGURE 8.11 If you're like most people, your eye zeroed in on the location circled in red. The white circle is too close to the edge of the square. Visual tension exists because the relationship between the square and circle is unbalanced.

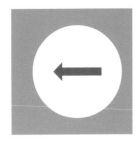

FIGURE 8.12 You can remove the visual tension by moving the circle further away from the square's edge, adding balance to the relationship.

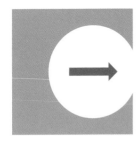

FIGURE 8.13 You can also remove the visual tension by moving the circle past the square's edge so it clearly overlaps it and improves the shape relationship.

The tension comes from the circle being too close to the edge of the green square. It unintentionally draws your eye to that area. To remedy this, you have to either move the circle further away from the edge, as shown in **FIGURE 8.12**, or move the circle past the edge, as shown in **FIGURE 8.13**. These are the fundamental design decisions you'll make every day as a designer.

Most successful designers are expert manipulators, practiced in the art of using composition to visually guide the viewer's eye through a design or to focus attention on a specific location within a given context. You want the viewer to give purposeful attention to important content and not be distracted by unnecessary elements or poor design decisions.

Bad design, in general, is riddled with visual tension. The more areas of visual tension within a graphic, the greater the risk of compromising the intended visual communication. It's crucial, as a self-art director, to recognize and remove visual tension from your artwork. And, as with anything, the first step in solving a problem is recognizing that you have one.

Recognize Visual Tension

Before jumping into a real-world project that contains visual tension, let's take a look at a common graphic that everyone is familiar with: the American flag. I think it's safe to say we've all seen this motif enough that we could spot anything in it that's not quite right.

If you look at **FIGURE 8.14**, you'll see a normal flag and one with a lot of visual tension. Your challenge is to pinpoint all 22 areas of visual tension in this graphic. Some problems are obvious, while others are much more subtle. In **FIGURE 8.15**, it may seem at first that all the issues have been remedied, but look more closely.

As a designer, you may sometimes intentionally mess up a graphic to achieve a certain look and feel. In that context, visual tension is thrown out the window. But that's the exception, not the rule. So, unless the genre specifically calls for a style that's loose, random, or chaotic in its composition, you should be mindful that visual tension is a negative attribute within a design.

FIGURE 8.14 There are a total of 22 areas of visual tension in the right flag graphic. Compare this with the left flag and see whether you can find all the areas where elements are distorted or positioned or scaled incorrectly.

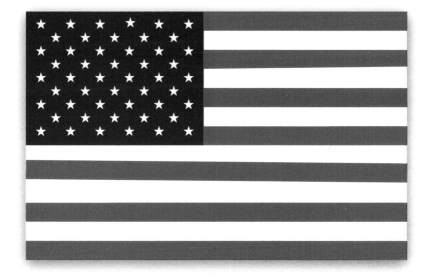

FIGURE 8.15 In this version of the flag graphic, I've corrected 19 of the 22 areas of visual tension. But three areas of subtle tension remain. Can you pinpoint them?

The flag samples demonstrate that visual tension can be both overt and subtle. The latter is obviously harder to spot, so you'll really need to train your eye to detect it.

Let's walk through a project in which I isolated several instances of visual tension so you can see how I resolved them.

FIGURE 8.16 The logotype contains numerous areas of visual tension.

When I added the various outlines to this hand-lettered logotype, it caused a lot of visual tension (**FIGURE 8.16**). Look closely and you'll see the following:

A. The descender of the "K" is too thin.

B. The "U" is sitting on the edge of the "K."

C. The "S" is touching the edge of the "U."

D. The "S" is obstructing too much of the "U."

E. There's too much space between the "S" and the "K."

F. Both arms of the "K" are too thin.

G. The "K" should overlap the "O."

H. The exclamation mark is too thin and short.

Visual tension can be caused by any sort of poorly handled shape relationship. Any time your eye is pulled toward an unintended area, it's a safe bet that there's some form of visual tension within the design.

Once I'd identified the areas of visual tension, I was able to fix them (**FIGURE 8.17**). Notice how I also fixed the awkward slivers of negative space created by the outlines surrounding the "U" and "S." When I added a bear character, I paid very close attention so as not to create new areas of visual tension (**FIGURE 8.18**).

FIGURE 8.17 Compare the before and after of this logotype. I removed all areas of visual tension as shown in the bottom sample to improve the readability of the design. Spotting visual tension may seem a bit foreign at first, but over time you'll be able to spot these problems quickly.

FIGURE 8.18 The final vector artwork used on packaging for a line of kid's snacks.

Full-Tilt Creative Boogie

If creativity has an antithesis, it has to be complacency.

To grow as a creative person, it's essential to leave your comfort zone, take design risks, apply new methods like the fresh eyes effect, and eliminate visual tension. All of this will help you develop new styles for yourself and your clients.

Realize that when you do these things, you're bound to fail, but those failures only add to your growth as a creative professional. You simply can't improve without trying and failing. So use T.N.T. (Try New Things) to blow up your creative norm.

Remember, art directing yourself means you need to be your own worst critic. Don't settle for good enough. Keep your creative standard high and relentlessly pursue design excellence so it becomes your natural creative penchant.

Resist taking the easy road toward design stagnation. Instead, stir up your creative juices and eventually you'll be doing the full-tilt creative boogie!

DESIGN DRILLS:
Hop to It

Nothing teaches methodology like redundancy. So, let's walk through yet another design project—this time, a character illustration called "Thug Bunny"—to help cement the vector creative process in your brain (**FIGURES 8.19 TO 8.39**).

FIGURE 8.19 I start by drawing out thumbnail sketches of the Thug Bunny character. Remember to step away from your computer at the beginning of the project and pick up pencil and paper. Sketching out your ideas before you head into Adobe Illustrator is essential to creating well-crafted vector art.

FIGURE 8.20 Drawing is a progressive medium, so I'm now dialing the character in more with a tighter rough sketch. I draw half of the art, scan it, and then flip it to gauge whether I'm moving in the right direction.

FIGURE 8.21 Using the tighter rough sketch as my guide, I now draw my refined sketch.

FIGURE 8.23 Here I'm doing rough building on the character's face. The only thing I'm concerned about is placing the anchor points in their correct positions. I proceed point by point (see Chapter 6, "Vector Build Methods").

FIGURE 8.24 With my anchor points in prime placement, I use the PathScribe plug-in to shape the Bézier curves, adjusting the handles so that the curves match those in the underlying sketch.

FIGURE 8.22 This is the finalized sketch, which I'll scan in and use to build my vector shapes. I'll rely on my good friend symmetry to complete the picture.

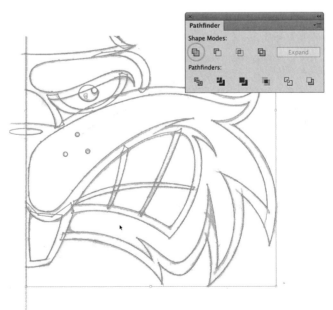

FIGURE 8.25 Notice how I dissect my design into smaller, more manageable shapes. Now I'll use the Pathfinder panel (Shift-Command-F9 or Shift-Control-F9) to unite my vector shapes. The Unite tool is circled in green.

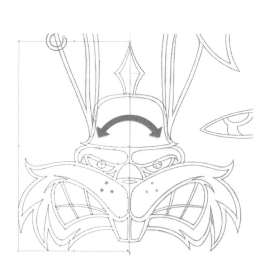

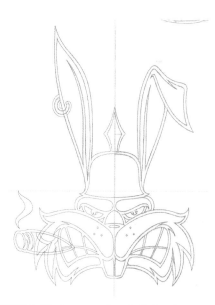

FIGURE 8.26 With the base vector shapes completed, I copy them and use the Reflect tool to flip them. (For more information on using symmetry, see Chapter 6.)

FIGURE 8.27 Once I've fused all the elements together, I'm ready to start filling in the design with black and white.

FIGURE 8.28 With the black and white filled in, I scrutinize my design, looking for areas to improve on. I usually print out the art and mark it up with a red pen, but on this project, I just zoomed in and scrutinized the artwork onscreen.

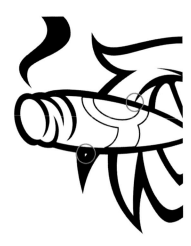

FIGURE 8.29 My inner art director spots two areas of visual tension (circled in orange).

FIGURE 8.30 I remove both areas of visual tension simply by moving the cigar shape down.

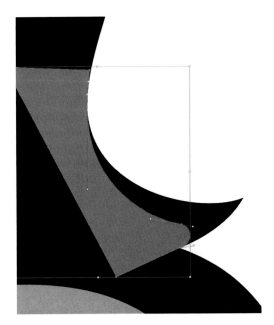

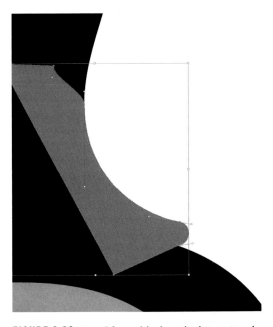

FIGURE 8.31 After walking away from the project for a few hours and returning with fresh eyes, I notice that the brim of the helmet comes to too much of a point, so I rebuild that shape (shown in green).

FIGURE 8.32 I modify my black-and-white art and unite this new piece (shown in green) to it via the Pathfinder panel. (For more information about Pathfinder, review Chapter 2, "Your Creative Armament.")

FIGURE 8.33 This shows the helmet before modification.

FIGURE 8.34 This shows the helmet after I've improved it.

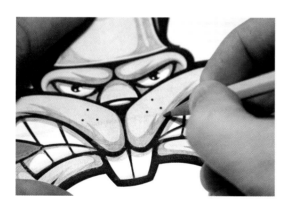

FIGURE 8.35 It's time to jump back into analog. At this point, I print out my character design in black and white and draw in the shading details using a 2B pencil.

FIGURE 8.36 I scan the drawn shading in and use it as a guide to build my new vector shapes.

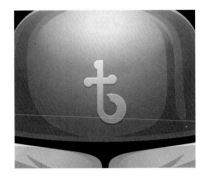

FIGURE 8.38 As I near the end of the project, I decide that the helmet looks too bare, so I create a unique logo mark. After all, Thug Bunny wouldn't be half as cool if he didn't have his own logo to emblazon on his *pickelhaube*.

FIGURE 8.37 Analog methods like this drawn shading improve digital workflows and make vector building easier.

FIGURE 8.39 Years ago, a colleague and I considered starting a new design firm. We developed potential names and the one we settled on was Thug Bunny. That creative partnership never came to fruition, but I loved the name so much that I decided to use it for this fun illustration.

CHAPTER 9

Basic Coloring and Detailing

The purpose of this book is to improve your core vector-building skills through a systematic creative process that starts with drawing and ends with the precise formation of vector paths in Adobe Illustrator. This chapter will help you expand on your core vector-building skills by using color and detailing in the context of a vector-based illustration.

How Light Affects Color

Before you jump into the use of color, it's important to understand the basic principles of light and how it affects color.

Simply put, without light you wouldn't have color. So, the absence of light means the absence of color. Artistically speaking, black is the complete absence of color. When you introduce light, you begin to introduce color. Think of the night sky—it's mostly black. But if the moon begins to reflect the sun, the light brings out additional hues; they may be muted or dark, but they're no longer distinctly black. And the closer they are to the brightness of the moon, the brighter they'll be.

You can approach your vector-coloring efforts in the same way. When all your base vector shapes are completely built and you start thinking about color, first consider your light source, what direction will it be coming from, and how it will affect the colors you choose.

A Pure White Light Source

A pure white light source interacts with shapes like these colored cubes (**FIGURE 9.1**) and gives them volume and form. Underneath each cube you'll see what I call tonal families, which I'll cover in more depth shortly.

A Warm or Cool Light Source

Not all light sources are pure white. **FIGURE 9.2** shows a warm light source interacting with the colored cubes. The hues of the cubes' colors are warmer now because they have more yellow and red added to them. A cool light source would introduce some blue, and the colors would have less yellow and red.

Whether you use a pure white, warm, or cool light source, the light interacts with the value of the color and helps to form the shape. The introduction of light isn't merely a visual aesthetic—the use of warm or cool colors helps to set the mood of your art, so keep that in mind as well.

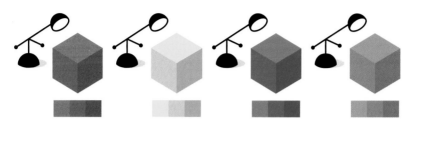

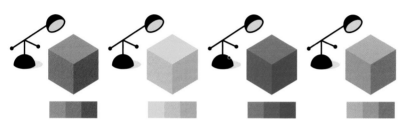

FIGURE 9.1 A pure white light source interacts with the cubes' colors to help shape and form them. Light gives the illusion of depth and begins forming detail.

FIGURE 9.2 A warm light source gives the specific hues of each cube a warmer overall feel.

Using Tonal Families

Before jumping into the process of coloring, I like to set up what I call *tonal families*. These are groups of color swatches associated with the same general hue (**FIGURE 9.3**).

At the least, a tonal family has three members: a base color, an intermediate color, and a shadow color. Beyond that, it can have a range of color iterations depending on your specific creative context. Be sure to make all the colors global colors (see more on this in Chapter 10, "Good Creative Habits," specifically Figure 10.30).

If you look through all the source files included with this book, you'll see that I use tonal families in each project. I highly recommend adding prefabricated tonal families to your new document profile so they're automatically included when you begin a new project. See Chapter 2, "Your Creative Armament," for more information about customizing your work environment.

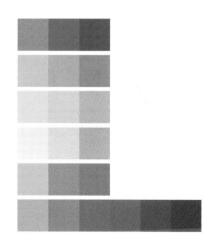

FIGURE 9.3 Using tonal families and global colors speeds up build times, helps you think through your creative process, and lets you work more efficiently.

Hierarchy of Color and Detail

 Coloring and detailing a vector design is a progressive process. As much as I try to systematize it, it's largely a process of creative discovery. And at times I'll struggle with figuring out how to handle color or detail in a specific area. This is normal and should be expected regardless of how experienced you are.

Creativity, vector or otherwise, is all about using trial and error to discover what works and what doesn't. You may discover something that will expand your skill set and help you on future work even though it doesn't apply to the current project.

Simplifying the Coloring Process

FIGURES 9.4–9.8 show the process of starting with base vector shapes (Figure 9.4), applying base colors to the vector shapes (Figure 9.5), adding shadow coloring detail (Figure 9.6), working out the highlight areas (Figure 9.7), and how this hierarchy of color works in the final illustration (Figure 9.8).

FIGURE 9.4 Tonal families assist me in my initial shape coloring. I start by selecting the base vector shape and then use the eyedropper tool (I) to select and apply the color to it. This is faster than going to the swatch palette all the time.

FIGURE 9.5 With the base colors established, I have a good idea of how the art will look. Next I begin to think through how the light source will influence the detail.

FIGURE 9.6 I add all the areas needing shading detail via the use of gradient fills and additional vector shapes with blend mode settings. From this point on, the process is experimental. For example, here I've made another on-the-fly decision to define the cheek using a unique shape and another gradient blend.

FIGURE 9.7 Adding highlights really begins to breathe life into the illustration. I use hard-edge highlights, as shown on the forehead and nose, as well as more subtle highlights, such as the radial gradient on the brow.

FIGURE 9.8 The various kinds of coloring work together with additional thematic detailing like the five o'clock shadow and the spots on the forehead.

Building Highlights and Shadows

There's an art and science to building highlights and shadows in vector format. Over the years I've developed several helpful methods that can be applied to any style of illustration. Feel free to adapt them to fit your own preferences—that's how you'll sustain your creativity over the long haul.

Using Black for Shading

FIGURE 9.9 shows how I used a linear gradient blending from 30% black to white. This gradient is set to the Multiply blend mode. I find the use of black for shading problematic in that it tends to look muddy. On lighter color schemes like this skin tone, it's especially noticeable.

Using Tonal Families for Shading

FIGURE 9.10 shows how I use a linear gradient blending from 35% of my darkest tonal family to white. This gradient is set to the Multiply blend mode. Using a darker tonal family produces a far better result than a tint of black does, especially on lighter colors like this.

Compare the black shading to the tonal family shading in the final orb composition. Which one do you think looks better?

FIGURE 9.9 Using black for shading is the lazy man's approach to shadowing, in my opinion. When a gradient like this is set to the Multiply blend mode, white appears transparent and won't show up. This is important to remember because you'll use this a lot in your coloring efforts moving forward.

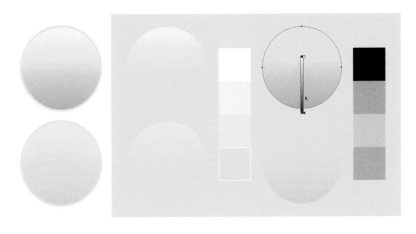

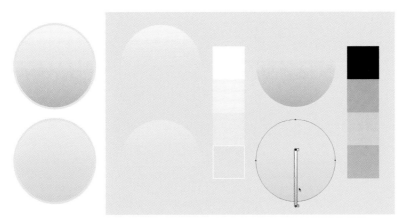

FIGURE 9.10 This shading color looks far more appealing than the black version. Once again, white becomes transparent since the blend mode is set to Multiply.

Using White for Highlights

FIGURE 9.11 shows a linear gradient blending from 50% white to the base color set at 0% opacity. You can adjust the percentage to make it more overt or subtle as you want. White can work on lighter colors, but for darker colors, white is a bit trickier to use.

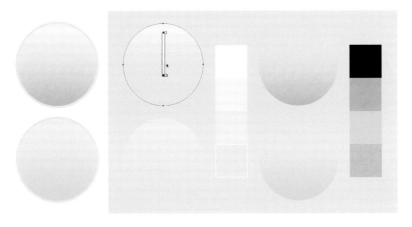

FIGURE 9.11 This highlighting on a light color is acceptable. Notice how the blend mode is set to Normal and the gradient blends to 0% opacity of the base color.

Using Tonal Families for Highlights

FIGURE 9.12 shows a linear gradient blending from 70% tint of the base color to 0% opacity of the base color. I find this approach works best on all colors, from light to dark.

Compare the white highlighting to the tonal family highlighting in the final orb composition. It's more graceful and elegant.

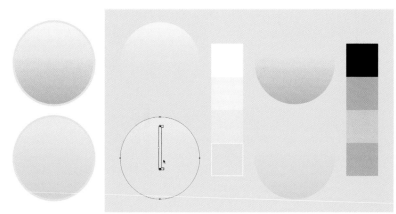

FIGURE 9.12 When it comes to detailing like this, there's no absolute right or wrong. Using black and white for shadows and highlights isn't incorrect; but, in my opinion, shadows and highlights look better when they're based on tonal families.

Comparing Other Color Usages

FIGURES 9.13 and **9.14** let you compare the use of black shadows and white highlights with equivalent tonal family applications. The darker the color, the more forgiving the use of black for shading will be. And using tonal families for highlights looks more authentic than using white.

Your preference will dictate your use of all of these, so take time to experiment and decide what you like best.

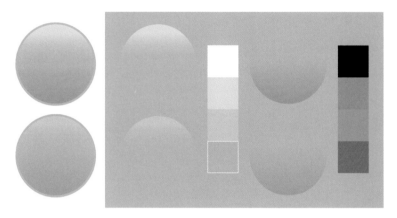

FIGURE 9.13 On a more neutral color like this green, both approaches look fine, although I still tend to gravitate toward tonal families in the final application.

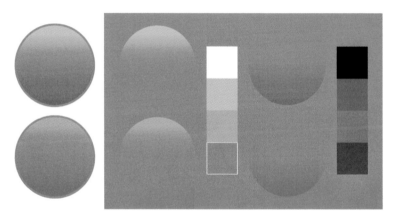

FIGURE 9.14 Black looks fine on a darker color like this red; I've used it on darker colors myself. But white looks clunky in its application. Tonal family gradients produce better highlights on a darker color like this and blend better as well.

Using Gradient Blends and Blend Modes

Many methods in Illustrator align or overlap with one another. You've already seen me use and apply gradients and blend modes to pull off various detailing such as shadows and highlights.

Gradients and blend modes can greatly enhance a vector illustration. It's all about using them wisely to achieve the specific look and feel you're after.

Getting Compelling Results

After you establish your base colors, you can use gradients to create dimension in your design. In **FIGURE 9.15**, I've adjusted a linear gradient to form the shading in one area of my tribal mask illustration using tonal families from dark to a lighter base color.

In **FIGURE 9.16**, I've positioned my gradient to create the highlighted area on the brow. Notice how it's blending to 0% opacity of the base color.

In **FIGURE 9.17**, I've made a copy of the outer profile shape and filled it with a radial gradient blending from the fire color out to 0% opacity of the base color. This shape sits on top of the overall illustration. In **FIGURE 9.18**, I've set the blend mode for this gradient to Overlay and the opacity of the shape to 60%. Notice how the gradient now interacts with the art below it.

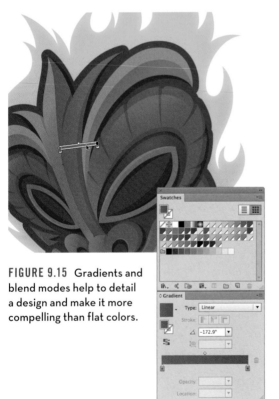

FIGURE 9.15 Gradients and blend modes help to detail a design and make it more compelling than flat colors.

FIGURE 9.16 Blending gradients to 0% opacity is an easy way to achieve subtle highlights.

The last radial gradient is an oval filled with the same blend from the fire color to 0% opacity of the base color. I set the blend mode to Hard Light and the opacity of the shape to 20% (**FIGURE 9.19**).

The use of gradients and blend modes in this design was a relatively simple task, yet the results are compelling (**FIGURE 9.20**).

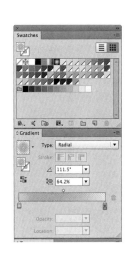

FIGURE 9.17 This process was a direct result of experimenting. I didn't originally plan on doing this, but because I took the time to try new things, I discovered a great detailing trick that I'll now use again.

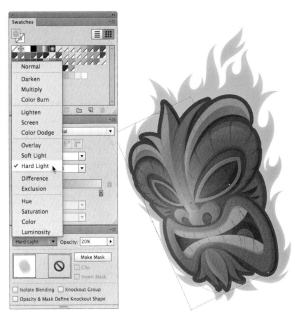

FIGURE 9.18 I remember thinking to myself when I clicked Overlay for the first time, "That rocks!" This one detailing trick adds a lot of life to the design.

FIGURE 9.19 If one is good, two is usually better. In this case, it really makes the effect believable. It looks like the glow from the fire is reflecting off the mask.

FIGURE 9.20 The final
Freaky Tiki tribal mask
illustration.

Deep Shadows and Hot Spots

General shading and highlights are great, but additional attention can enhance these details and really push your design over the top. I refer to these more subtle details as *deep shadows* and *hot spots*.

Deep Shadows

Lurking in most shadows are even darker areas that add dimension and interest. In **FIGURE 9.21**, base colors and initial shadows and highlights are already established. The illustration looks good, but adding some darker areas of shading will improve it even more. Compare Figure 9.21 with **FIGURE 9.22**, where I've added in deep shadows to the top edge of the eyelid and the cast shadow as it overlaps the eye.

Hot Spots

Hot spots are areas where a highlight is the hottest and brightest. In **FIGURE 9.23**, I've added hot spots to the brow above the eye, nose, gill, and pupil. These are usually the last bits of detailing I do.

While these effects are subtle, when handled well, they can really make the difference in a design, as shown in **FIGURE 9.24**.

FIGURE 9.21 No hot spots or deep shadows.

FIGURE 9.22 Deep shadows added to illustration.

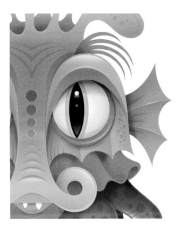

FIGURE 9.23 Hot spots added to illustration.

FIGURE 9.24 Final Amphiblien illustration.

Spot Detailing with Radial Gradients and Layering

Using simple features in Illustrator like radial gradients and layering is key to adding effective details to your illustrations. Don't limit your use of them to the techniques I show you in this chapter; experiment and find other ways to apply them in your vector artwork.

Organized Chaos

As you colorize your vector artwork, your process might become messy. The following techniques will help you keep your creative process simple and organized.

FIGURE 9.25 shows how detailing adds a nice level of dimension and interest to this character illustration. My process involves adding many carefully placed radial gradients organized via layers (Figure 9.25). When you isolate the specific layers that contain the radial gradients, they look like a jumbled mess, but the organized chaos builds up the tonal values and details I need.

FIGURE 9.25 Well-placed radial gradients combined with organized layering help to create a compelling monster character illustration.

FIGURES **9.26** and **9.27** show the adjustments I'm making to the color, opacity, size, angle, and blend mode setting of each radial gradient. I'm adding these as I build and sandwiching them on top of and behind vector shapes to create the look and feel I want.

The organized, layered content gives me direct access to all parts of the illustration (**FIGURE 9.28**). This lets me scrutinize my detailing, make adjustments, and recompile content as necessary until I've achieved the exact look I'm after (**FIGURE 9.29**). For more information and examples of layering, see Chapter 10.

FIGURE 9.26 Isolated on their own, radial gradients look strange and out of place. But in the context of background colors and shapes, they merge to form an effective detailing method.

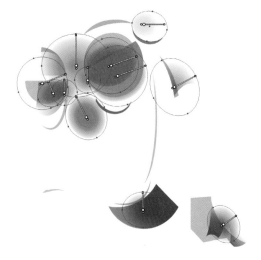

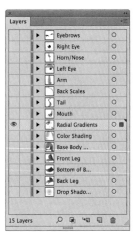

FIGURE 9.27 The settings of each radial gradient help me achieve the specific look needed for the area where the gradient is being used. The selected shape in this image is a darker hue of the base color set to the Multiply blend mode and 90% opacity.

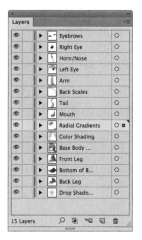

FIGURE 9.28 Layers are your friends, so don't ignore them—use them wisely. And when you use them, take the time to name each one appropriately.

FIGURE 9.29 The final monster character illustration. This figure's name is Snilbog.

Inner and Outer Glow and Gaussian Blur Effects

Illustrator has several powerful features that utilize Photoshop-type effects in a vector-based environment. Inner and outer glow and Gaussian blur are three methods of detailing that let you apply raster-based effects to your vector shapes (think pixels). These methods can greatly enhance an illustration when applied creatively.

Applying Inner Glows

To create the inner glow effect, first select the vector shape you want to apply it to; then go to the navigation menu at the top of the screen and select Effect > Style > Inner Glow (**FIGURE 9.30**).

The iconic gear head illustration shown in Figure 9.30 has a dark gray inner glow, with the blend mode set to Multiply, the opacity set to 45%, and the blur size set to 10 pt. The final size of your illustration will determine your specific settings.

Applying Outer Glows

To access the outer glow effect, first select the vector shape you want to apply it to; then go to the navigation menu at the top of the screen and select Effect > Style > Outer Glow (**FIGURE 9.31**).

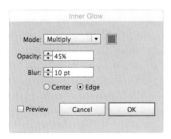

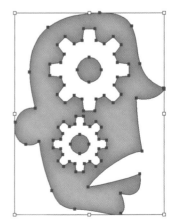

FIGURE 9.30 Inner glow applied to a gear head illustration.

The iconic angler fish illustration shown in Figure 9.31 has a yellow outer glow, with the blend mode set to Normal, the opacity set to 100%, and the blur size set to 10 pt. Once again, the exact settings you use will be determined by your design's final size.

Applying Gaussian Blur

To access the Gaussian blur effect, first select the vector shape you want to apply it to; then go to the navigation menu at the top of the screen and select Effect > Blur > Gaussian Blur (**FIGURE 9.32**).

The iconic character illustration shown in Figure 9.32 has a Gaussian blur radius of 14 pixels applied to the blue color shape. Like inner and outer glow effect, you'll want to pick a blur radius based on your artwork's final size. Remember that your document's raster effects resolution setting will affect how this effect appears; you can set yours by choosing Effects > Document Raster Effects Settings.

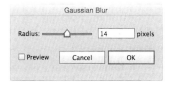

FIGURE 9.31 Outer glow applied to an angler fish illustration.

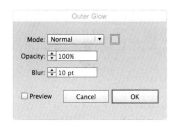

FIGURE 9.32 Gaussian blur applied to a character illustration.

FIELD NOTES

Pay Attention to the Details

Get in the creative habit of analyzing artwork you see and admire. I am not just talking digital work; study illustrators of the past as well. Look at how they handle their detailing. How did they shade or add highlights? What methods can you discern in their work?

Observing illustrative cues like this and adapting them to your own workflow is how you grow and morph your own creative process and improve your core skills.

Over time you'll discover your own unique ways of handling detail, which is the whole point of paying attention to detail now.

Endless Creative Possibilities

There are so many variables and illustrative styles that it's impossible to cover everything regarding coloring and detail in one book. I've only scratched the surface and have given you a basic methodology that you can now expand on as you move forward.

For more information about the use of color and detailing methods, check out my "Drawing Vector Graphics: Color and Detail" course at www.DrawingVectorGraphics.com.

DESIGN DRILLS:
Using Effects in Illustrative Detailing

Effects such as blurs and glows are great, but they're often overused or just poorly applied. The last thing you want is for the effect to grab more attention than the illustration itself. Knowing when and how to use effects and balance their aesthetic so they enhance, rather than detract from, your composition is important.

FIGURE 9.33 shows a composition with all my final vector shapes and use of color. It doesn't look bad; it just looks very flat and lacks dimension.

This design is ideal to show how to apply the glow and Gaussian blur effects to some of the vector shapes to improve the overall look and feel of the illustration. I'll start by applying the inner and outer glow (**FIGURES 9.34–9.38**).

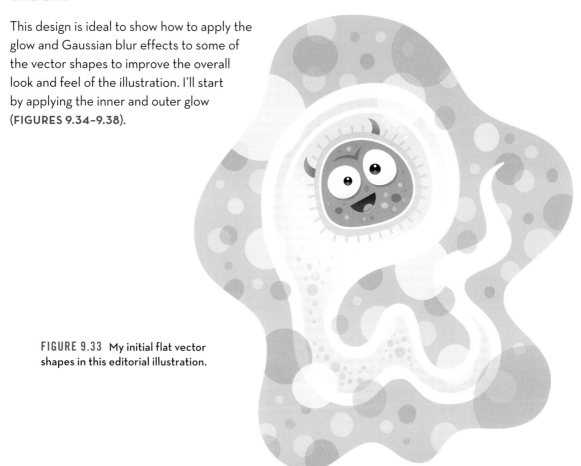

FIGURE 9.33 My initial flat vector shapes in this editorial illustration.

FIGURE 9.34 I can enhance my genetic character's creative DNA using the inner glow effect.

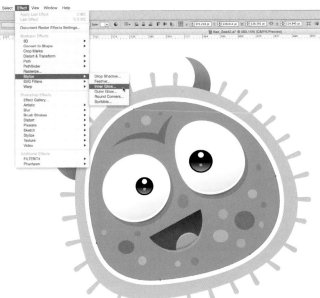

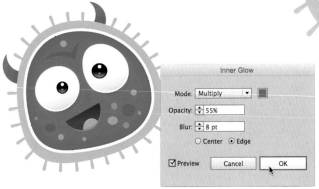

FIGURE 9.35 I've applied an inner glow effect of a darker green to the character. The blend mode is set to Multiply, the opacity is set to 55%, and the blur is set to 8 pt.

FIGURE 9.36 I can apply other inner and outer glows to additional shapes in the illustration.

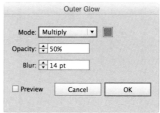

FIGURE 9.37 Here I've applied an outer glow effect of a darker green. The blend mode is set to Multiply, the opacity is set to 50%, and the blur is set to 14 pt.

FIGURE 9.38 I've now applied all the inner and outer glows to the vector shapes in the design.

Next I'll apply Gaussian blur effects to some of the vector shapes (**FIGURES 9.39** and **9.40**). The result drastically improves the illustration. There's a nice level of dimension to the artwork, and it's now far more interesting visually (**FIGURE 9.41**).

FIGURE 9.39 I can improve the background shape by applying a Gaussian blur to the free-floating orbs.

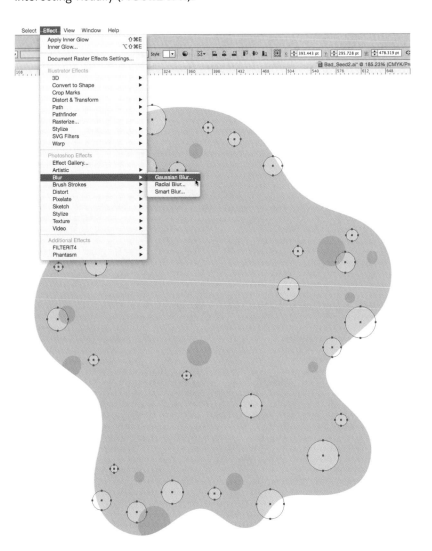

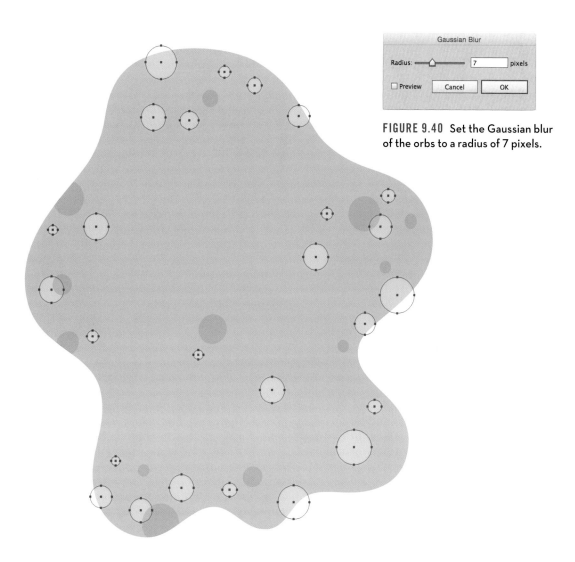

FIGURE 9.40 Set the Gaussian blur of the orbs to a radius of 7 pixels.

Compare the final results shown in Figure 9.41 with the original flat shape in Figure 9.33. The effects have made the final artwork far more interesting. That should always be your goal when using effects like this. So, take time to experiment with them and combine them with other methods described in this book. You'll discover even more ways to use them in your own work.

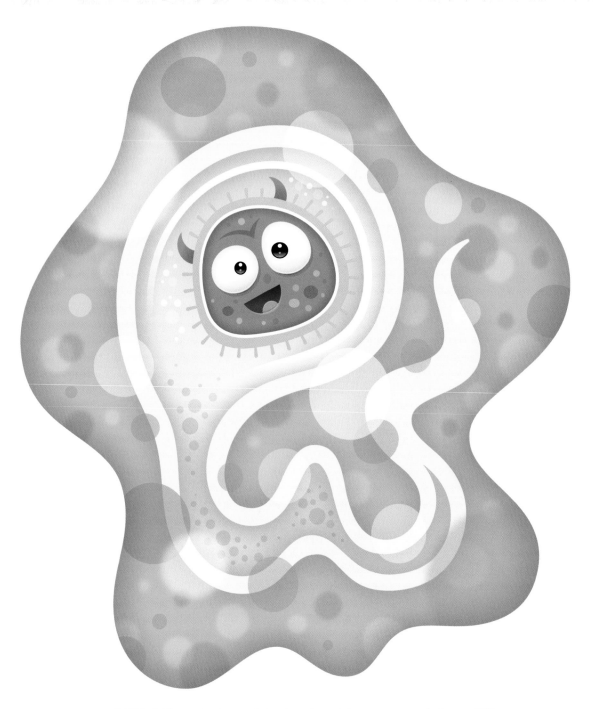

FIGURE 9.41 The final artwork for this editorial illustration on nefarious cloning shows how the use of effects can greatly improve an illustration.

CHAPTER 10

Good
Creative Habits

Whether you're a designer or an illustrator, you're expected to deliver creativity on a daily basis. It doesn't matter if you're in the mood to create. You rarely have the luxury of waiting until inspiration strikes to move forward on a design project.

So, how do you stay on creative high alert, fully prepared to meet your daily design challenges? The answer is simple: Establish good creative habits (**FIGURE 10.1**).

Good creative habits help to increase productivity, improve efficiency, raise quality, fuel creative passion, ignite inspiration, bring about new creative opportunities, cure cancer, solve homelessness, and establish everlasting peace on Earth. OK, well, maybe not those last three things.

In this chapter, I'll share several creative habits that I use regularly and find effective. In addition to these, you should always be on the hunt for

FIGURE 10.1 The good creative habit of doodling can be leveraged as final art, as shown in this editorial illustration called "Digital Lifestyle."

creative habits that are specific to *your* work. Strive to continually establish good creative habits, and your well of inspiration will never run dry.

> "A moment's insight is sometimes worth a life's experience."
> —OLIVER WENDELL HOLMES

Doodle Binders

All designers should draw—period.

The systematic creative processes that I've documented throughout this book all illustrate the importance of sound drawing skills in building precise vector graphics. And in Chapter 3, "Analog Methods in a Digital Age," I show how drawing can help you better formulate ideas and expand your creative potential. That's not to say that all designers should strive to be illustrators. But doodling on a regular basis is a great way to flex those drawing muscles and develop them into a new and powerful part of your creative approach. Draw, draw, draw—everywhere, anywhere, all the time.

The first creative habit that I want you to add to your routine is doodling. Doodling works best when done spontaneously, without any purpose. That said, to sustain and capture this type of random creative energy, you need to plan ahead. Here are some simple things you can do to establish effective doodling skills.

1. **Keep pen and paper handy:** Whether it's a Moleskin sketchbook or just a notepad, keep it next to you at work, in your living room, in your car, when you travel, next to the phone, in your purse, and so on. You need to be able to draw at a moment's notice. As long as you have a pen, though, you can draw on anything **(FIGURE 10.2)**.

FIGURE 10.2 You can draw on almost any surface. My daughter Savannah made good use of this Styrofoam cup. (Of course, I take full genetic credit for this creativity.)

2. **Save your doodles:** Whenever you draw a new doodle, make sure you save it. I cut mine out of the paper I draw them on (I prefer doodling on notepads) and file them in what I call my doodle folder (**FIGURE 10.3**).

FIGURE 10.3 I save all my doodles—no matter what I draw them on—and keep them in a designated doodle folder until I need them.

3. **Archive your doodles:** When your doodle folder nears overflowing, it's time to move your doodles to a more permanent home. I take the ones I've collected, paste them on regular bond paper, slide them into plastic sleeves, and insert these pages into a doodle binder.

FIGURE 10.4 I archive my collected doodles in binders for easy reference and safekeeping. The binders are also a great resource for inspiration.

Over a period of time, you can create an incredible doodle reference library that documents your spontaneous inspiration. My own doodle binders date back over twenty years now, and when I look through them, I relive the creative thoughts I had at that time (**FIGURE 10.4**). These binders have enabled me to use ideas that I would've otherwise forgotten long ago.

Besides the practical benefits of doodling and saving your doodles, it's also a whole lot of fun to draw in this manner! An excellent resource is my friend Mike Rohdes' book *The Sketchnote Handbook,* which will help you develop your doodling skills and use them to enhance your cognitive abilities.

Layers Are Your Friend

I love teaming up with other designers on creative projects. The brainstorming and conceptual partnership involved in working together toward a common goal makes for a great experience, and, more importantly, it results in incredible design solutions.

The proverbial fly in this collaborative ointment for me, however, is the difference in our creative habits—specifically how other designers organize their files and manage their graphic content.

By the time a fellow designer sends me his or her final art, I'm not surprised by how it looks since I've seen comps during the collaborative process. What I need at that point is access to the vector art files.

Often when I open up the illustration file, however, I see vector art that, while it looks good to the naked eye, is horribly built. In this case, using this artwork isn't just difficult; it's painful.

I admit that I'm a bit uptight when it comes to my file management, but there really is no excuse for not using layers and for failing to organize vector content properly. That's just lazy building, which begets trouble down the road.

What type of trouble? Here are a few problematic scenarios that nonlayered design files can cause:

- **Build time:** If you layer your design as you progress with each new part of the whole, you'll save yourself a lot of time later hunting and pecking to isolate content within the design. Using layers not only speeds up your build time, but it makes any later editing far easier. Using layers also gives you better control over vector blend mode hierarchy, so you can get the visual effect you're after. (For more on layering and how it assists in organizing and utilizing blend modes, deconstruct the resource file for Chapter 6, "Vector Build Methods," called "Tickles the Evil Clown.")

- **Clutter:** Avoiding layers suggests that you're trying to see everything all the time as you create your vector design. This can become a distraction on a complex project. Being able to focus on a specific element within your design, without other content getting in the way, is essential. If you use layers, accessing only the elements you need at any given time will be less confusing because you can simply toggle content layers on and off as needed. You can also lock specific layers if you need the content visible but not selectable.

- **Repurposing:** It's a huge hassle to reuse unlayered vector art in future work. Trying to pinpoint specific vector shapes and select them will be frustrating. You also run the risk of missing some of the necessary content when you try to copy vector art to another file because some crucial items might be hiding under an element you're not copying. Layering content helps you avoid these types of problems. (Adobe Illustrator has a drill-down mode using the Direct Selection tool [A + Command key], but I have found its performance to be unreliable, so good layering is still critical.)

- **Retrieval:** How many pieces of art do you create in a given year? Will you remember exactly how you constructed a complex design when you open the file five years later? More than likely, you won't, and you'll waste time trying to deconstruct the art in order to use it. Layering the art properly lets you see exactly how the work was built and compiled into its final composition.

As you create your design, think of logical ways to organize your vector content. This will help you build files that are easy to navigate so you can quickly find the vector elements you need.

Let's take a look at a caricature project and see how layering plays a vital role in the overall creative process (**FIGURES 10.5–10.16**).

FIGURE 10.5 Thumbnail sketch for a caricature of President Barack Obama.

FIGURE 10.6 Now that my refined symmetrical caricature is done, I'll scan it in and move from analog to digital, building my vector shapes on top of the sketch in Illustrator. (For more information on drawing, review Chapter 3, "Analog Methods in a Digital Age." For more information about using symmetry, review Chapter 6.)

FIGURE 10.7 I'll use both the Point-by-Point Method (shown at top) and the Shape-Building Method (shown below) to create my vector art.

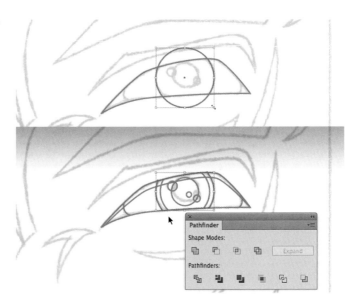

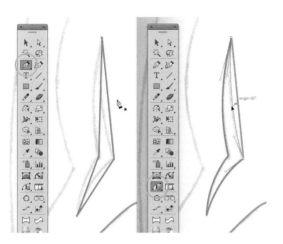

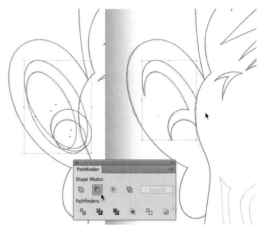

FIGURE 10.8 Wherever there's a point in the drawing, I place an anchor point using the Pen tool as shown at left. (Review the Point-by-Point Method in Chapter 6.) From this rough-built shape I now switch to the VectorScribe plug-in PathScribe tool and bend the path segments to match the underlying refined sketch as shown at right. You can use the Direct Selection tool (A) to distort segments on a path as well, but I prefer the plug-in. See Chapter 2, "Your Creative Armament," for more information.

FIGURE 10.9 Any time I can use a shape tool like the Ellipse tool (L) to create my content with precision, I do so because it's faster than the Point-by-Point Method on these types of geometric shapes.

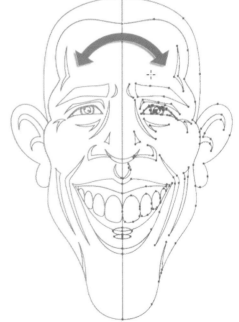

FIGURE 10.10 Since this artwork is symmetrical, I have to build only half of the vector content. Once that's done, I just copy and reflect it. (Review "Symmetry Is Your Friend" in Chapter 6.)

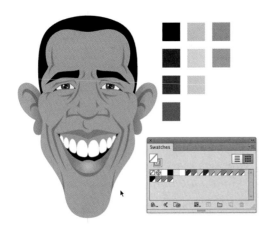

FIGURE 10.11 With the base vector shapes finished, I start to work out the colors. I might think about color earlier than this, but I avoid any actual color work until I have the form of all my shapes established. I also start to organize my file using layers.

FIGURE 10.12 It's time to move away from the computer now. I'll print it out and move back to analog, drawing out the shapes that will form my shading detail. Like my base shapes, this drawing will guide my vector building. (Review Chapter 3 for more on this back-and-forth process.)

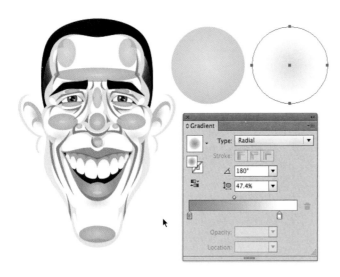

FIGURE 10.13 On an illustration like this, I use a lot of radial gradients. Using layers makes adjusting and altering them far easier. (For more information on using gradients for spot detailing, see Chapter 9.)

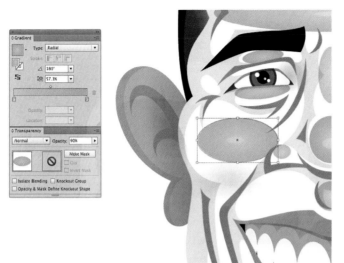

FIGURE 10.14 Keeping the radial gradients on their own layer makes fine-tuning the blend modes easier. I can arrange each layer in the layering hierarchy so that it works well with the design. In this illustration, I keep them below the vector shapes for the face shading. (To fully appreciate the flexibility afforded by layering, deconstruct the file called "Obama" included in the resource files.)

FIGURE 10.15 Using layers helps me keep track of all the detailing elements in an illustration. Being able to isolate content and turn layers on and off at will helps focus my attention on detail and allows me to achieve the visual look and feel I want.

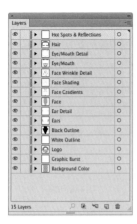

FIGURE 10.16 The final caricature design titled "Head of State." It would have been a major headache trying to build this design with everything on the same layer. Note in the Layers palette how I've logically ordered the content and labeled each layer to clearly define what it contains. If I open this file up four years from now, I won't have to guess how I layered the vectors. Using an organized layering system is a good creative habit that you'll appreciate more and more every year.

How to Avoid the Basement

All vector-building programs have layers. Within Adobe Illustrator, there are two types of layers. To help you understand both types, think of your drawing as a house that has a ground floor—your living area—and a scary basement. The ground floor is like the top-level layer in Illustrator. The basement is equivalent to the sublayer (**FIGURE 10.17**).

Illustrator automatically creates sublayers; you can't avoid it. Every layer has a sublayer; fortunately, you should never have to go there.

- **Top-level layer:** If you layer your vector designs using common sense, as described earlier, you'll rarely, if ever, have to go into the sublayers. Naming your top levels appropriately will obviously help you find your way around in your design, too.

- **Sublayers:** Whatever top-level layer you're building on, Illustrator will automatically create the sublayers for it. You should rarely have to drill down into that basement. But it's important to be aware that sublayers exist, regardless of whether you ever use them. (FYI: Adobe engineers call these layers the *object stack*.)

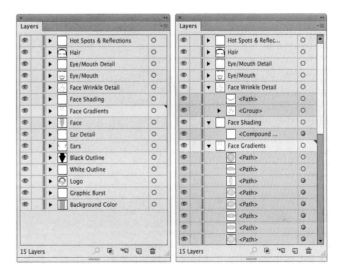

FIGURE 10.17 Think of your top-level layers as your living space. The sublayer is the scary basement. Consider the Obama illustration again. The top-level layering is shown on the left, and the sublayers that each of the top-level layers contain are waterfalled out on the right—scary! But as long as you have your top-level layering organized, there's really no reason to dive any deeper into the sublayers.

Combining Build Methods with Layering

In Chapter 6 you learned how dissecting vector shapes into smaller, more manageable pieces can help you construct a larger whole. You can apply that same principle to the composition of your entire design.

Some projects just work best if you handle them in a modular fashion. In this next example, I broke one project into two pieces—foreground and background—so I could better focus on the specifics of each. Later, I combined them to form one composition. I really had to depend on smart layering to manage all the detail and make controlling my vector graphics easier (**FIGURES 10.18–10.28**).

FIGURE 10.18 A thumbnail sketch for a Japanese-inspired repeat pattern design that will form the background of my final illustration.

FIGURE 10.19 My refined sketch for the repeat pattern design. Since the blossom shapes are so geometric, I don't need to waste time drawing them out precisely. I can easily create them using precise tools like the Ellipse tool (L).

FIGURE 10.20 I can create all the vines and leaves using The Clockwork Method (TCM) and Prime Point Placement (PPP) via the Point-by-Point Method (see Chapters 5 and 6). I can create the rest of the content using the Shape-Building Method (see Chapter 6). I now have all of the base vector shapes that will form the final pattern motif.

FIGURES 10.21—10.22 Using layers, I create a three-level hierarchy. Each is set to various transparencies to achieve the visual aesthetic that I'm after. The tile for my repeat pattern design is now complete (shown at right). For more information about creating your own repeat patterns, see my course "Drawing Vector Graphics: Patterns" at www.DrawingVectorGraphics.com.

FIGURE 10.23 Since this is the first time I'm illustrating in this style, I'll spend about a day refining my sketch so I can build my vector shapes on top of it as precisely as possible. I'll use lots of photo references to guide my drawing decisions along the way.

FIGURE 10.24 I need to use the Point-by-Point Method to build most of this illustration to achieve the specific look I'm going for. I'll use the Shape-Building Method only for the pupils of the eyes, since they're circular in shape. I'll use TCM and PPP for every other freeform vector shape. Notice how I dissect the vector shapes into smaller, more manageable pieces. (You can review all these methods in Chapters 5 and 6.)

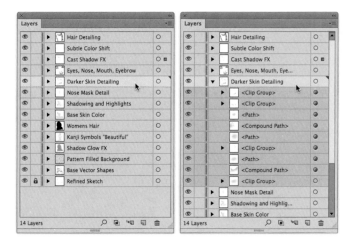

FIGURE 10.25 As I create this artwork, I organize the content using top-level layers only, as shown at left. Illustrator, of course, automatically creates the numerous sublayers shown at right.

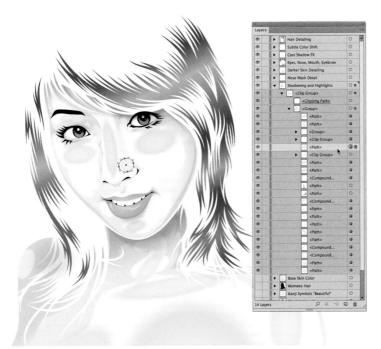

FIGURE 10.26 If you organize your top-level layers well, you'll never need to drill down into the sublayers. To do so, however, simply click the gray triangle on the top-level layer and the sublayers will flow below it (indented). The sublayers on a complex illustration like this could number in the hundreds and even contain additional hierarchical sublayers within them. If you choose to go into the basement of your art, it can get pretty cluttered and confusing, as shown in the box at left.

FIGURE 10.27 If you take the time to arrange your top-level layers coherently and name them in a way that tells you what each one is, then you can avoid navigating the needless process bloat that is sublayers.

FIGURE 10.28 I combine the repeat pattern design and my illustration into one unified composition to form my final illustration called "Beautiful." The good creative habit of layering made the creative process a lot easier and faster.

Colors and File Naming

When it comes to using colors and naming files, the system you choose depends more on your personal preference than anything else. But it's important to set up a system since you deal with colors and file naming every day.

When you work digitally, the more you can automate routine functions and set preferences, the more efficient and easier your workflow will become.

When it comes to color swatches in Illustrator, it's smart to create a custom set of colors that you use on a regular basis so you don't have to re-create the wheel each time you work on a new project. I call these sets of colors *tonal families*. (See Chapter 9, "Basic Coloring and Detailing," for more information on tonal families.)

It's simple: Just add your preferred colors to your Swatches palette, double-click the swatch, and make sure to check the Global box (**FIGURE 10.29**). This makes using your selected colors, as well as performing universal or global edits of your preferred palette, quick and easy. If you don't click the Global box, you'll have to manually select every vector shape iteration that uses the color you want to change, one at a time, and then apply a new color to it. It's easy to overlook content when you work like that, but with global colors, making these types of color edits is easy.

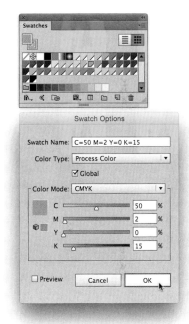

FIGURE 10.29 Every artist has specific color swatch preferences. My projects often require flesh tones, so I've included those. Any colors you find yourself using over and over again are good candidates for tonal families.

I arrange the tonal families in my color swatches so they run from light to dark. This makes selecting the right color faster than looking through a random assortment of color swatches when I build my designs.

Once you've created your custom set of color swatches, you can add it to your start-up profile so it's automatically included in every new document you open (also review "Create a New Document Profile" in Chapter 2).

A Typical Project Folder

Digital artists work with electronic files every day. On my studio work-station alone, I have 990,503 individual files, and these files are found in 241,317 folders. It goes without saying that having a naming standard to keep track of your work will make finding specific files a whole lot easier.

Project_Name_Build.ai   Project_Name_Comp_v1.ai

Project_Name ƒ.ai   Project_Name_Whatever.ai

FIGURE 10.30 This image shows how I name my files. Project_Name_Build.ai contains all my build elements for every direction provided. If I need to harvest an element later, I access this file. Project_Name_Comp_v1.ai is what I present to clients for each direction so they can pick one for approval. Project_Name ƒ.ai is the final art. I use this same hierarchical standard for every variation of a project that has its own file.

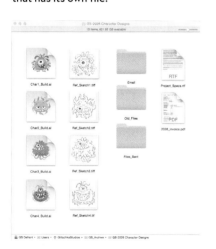

I wish someone would have clued me in on this back in the mid-1990s when I started archiving my work. It would have saved me a lot of time over the years, when I was fruitlessly looking for longforgotten file names and never finding the vector art I knew I had somewhere in my archive.

As shown in **FIGURE 10.30**, my file naming is methodical, and I keep it simple to aid in my future searches. As shown in **FIGURE 10.31**, a typical Glitschka Studios project folder contains the following:

- **_Build:** The staging, exploration, and building area for my vector creative work and typography

- **Ref_Sketch:** Drawn designs that I place in Illustrator so I can build on top of them

- **Project_Specs:** Compiled notes and information for quick reference

- **Email:** Key correspondence between the client and me

- **Old_Files:** Creative briefs, secondary documents, reference material, research, unicorns, and so on

- **Files_Sent:** Presentation, comps, and final art files

- **Invoice:** PDF of my project invoice sent to client

FIGURE 10.31 This image shows a typical project folder at Glitschka Studios. The project number in the folder name corresponds with the invoicing system I've established with my CPA to track job invoices I send out. Since all my projects use this type of formatting, I know exactly where to look to find content, whether it was a project I worked on three days ago or three years ago.

All of these are nested within a project folder that's labeled with a project number and name for archiving and backup purposes.

Creating color swatches and maintaining naming conventions aren't what I'd consider creative work, but they're good creative habits that will facilitate your workflow and give you more time to focus on what you'd rather be doing. In that respect, it's worth the initial investment to get your creative house in order.

Last but Not Least

Nothing will benefit you more as a design professional than establishing, practicing, and relentlessly refining your creative process. The benefits of doing so will be self-evident. The systematic creative processes documented in this book can greatly assist you in this regard.

But you know yourself best, and you know your bad creative habits. So I ask you, from this moment forward, to resist the urge to be a tooler (review Chapter 3), and pursue your career with design excellence at the forefront of your mind. Be purposeful in your dedication to creating quality art and producing your ideas with precision in vector form.

Set aside the bad creative habits that hold you back, and implement the methods and insights I've shared. Review your processes often to hold yourself accountable. Add good habits to your workflow, adapt them, improve them, and make them your own so you can create and grow in ways you've never known before.

Here endeth the lesson.

"Failure is not fatal, but failure to change might be."
—JOHN WOODEN

FIELD NOTES

VBT Wants You!

The learning process should never end. It's important to continually strive to grow in your creative pursuits, and there's no better way of doing this than to share your knowledge with others.

After you've read through this book and watched all of the videos, I encourage you to join the *Drawing Vector Graphics* Facebook group. This is where I share inspiring links, helpful information, creative rants, and artwork. And you'll be able to share your own methods, insights, and creative good habits with others in the design community so we can all benefit.

Join the Facebook group at www.facebook.com/DrawingVectorGraphics.

DESIGN DRILLS:
Top-Ten List

One of the hardest questions I'm asked as a creative professional is, "What's your favorite piece of artwork?" My usual answer: "The piece I'm working on right now." Truth be told, I get tired of my own work pretty quickly.

I hope you enjoy all of the artwork used in this book, but more importantly, I hope the methods I've shared with you will help you enjoy creating your own work even more (**FIGURES 10.32–10. 41**).

FIGURE 10.32 This owl will always have a special place in my heart because it was the first illustration of mine to be accepted by the New York Society of Illustrators. Having my work hang on the same walls as work by Norman Rockwell (one of my creative heroes) is just too stinking cool.

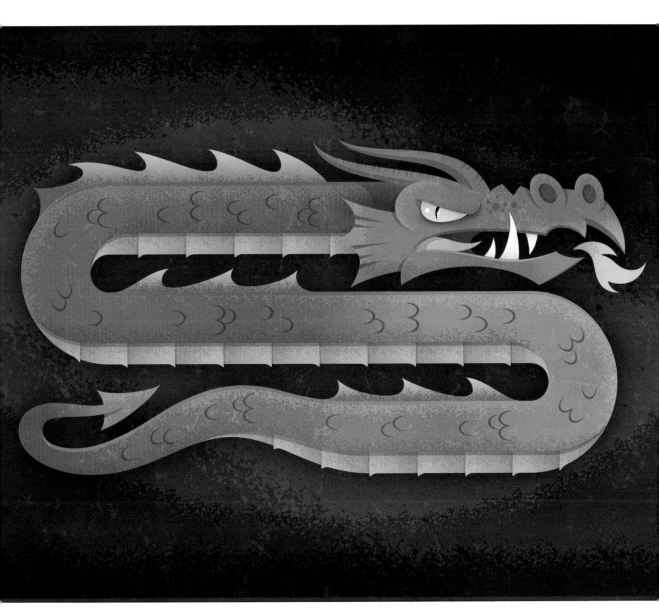

FIGURE 10.33 This dragon appeared on a splash screen for Adobe Creative Cloud (you might have seen it pop up on your screen when you open Illustrator). I used pattern brushes to do all the detailing. For more information about this type of detailing, see my course "Drawing Vector Graphics: Color and Detail" at DrawingVectorGraphics.com.

FIGURE 10.34 Sometimes I create a piece of art and when I'm done I have no idea why I created it or what it really means. That kind of happened here. When I was done, the title "Temporal Infestation" came to mind, and that made perfect sense to me. I also ran this art out as a large-format fine art print, and it hung in a local gallery for a few years as well.

FIGURE 10.35 The beauty of illustration is that you can defy reality in a fun way, as I did in this "Surf Safari" drawing for a children's book. I used the same pattern brushes as shown in Figure 10.33; it's also featured in my course.

FIGURE 10.36 This illustration accompanied a magazine article about the health benefits of walking. I picked a fun, linear style to reflect the theme of movement and activity, letting the continuous line form each of the walking figures in the composition.

FIGURE 10.37 I love vector artwork. I also love textures. When you combine the two, you can create wonderfully compelling visual narratives with an authentic, organic flair as shown in this illustration titled "Interlude." For more information about using textures with your vector art, see my "Creating and Using Textures for Design" course at www. DrawingVectorGraphics.com.

"Outside of a Dog, a Book is a Man's Best Friend. Inside of a Dog, it's too Dark to Read."

– Groucho Marx

FIGURE 10.38 Illustrative design can take many forms, one of which is illustrative hand lettering. I took one of my all-time favorite quotes and illustrated it for my "Drawing Vector Graphics: Hand Lettering" course at www.DrawingVectorGraphics.com.

FIGURE 10.39 Using real-world textures in design brings humanity to vector art. This artwork looks like it was traditionally painted, but in reality it's completely vector based. I hand painted textures and turned them into brushes to give this cat illustration an authentic look and feel. You'll find the brush set included in the resource files.

FIGURE 10.40 Can you tell yet that I like using textures? This graphic illustrative approach was for an editorial titled "Burning Conscience."

FIGURE 10.41 Ironically, the last illustration in this book utilizes none of the vector build methods I cover in this book. That's because I drew this artwork out in analog using a Paper Mate Flair marker and then image traced it in Illustrator. This was an experiment, and I love the results. It also shows that analog facilitates digital. So, never stop drawing—you never know where it'll take you, creatively speaking.

Index